D0883427

The Great Fur Opera

Annals of the Hudson's Bay Company 1670-1970

The Great Fur Opera
Annals of the Hudson's Bay Company 1670-1970

By Ronald Searle & Kildare Dobbs

 McClelland and Stewart limited : Toronto / Montreal

The Canadian Publishers
McClelland and Stewart Limited
25 Hollinger Road, Toronto 374

PRINTED AND BOUND IN CANADA

Contents

WARNING

What Mr. Dobbs has thought fit to call
a discription of Hudson's Bay, is so erronius,
so superficial, and so trifling in almost
every circumstance. . . .

Remarks of Captain W. Coats (1727–1751)

To the Honourable the Governor
   and
Company of Adventurers of England
  Trading into Hudson's Bay

Honourable Sirs,

  As the following little travesty was undertaken at your request and expense, it is no less my duty than my desire to dedicate it to you. Since you have seen fit to revive the lost custom of private literary patronage, it falls to me to restore the forgotten art of writing fulsome acknowledgement.

  For three hundred years Your Honours have directed a Company uniquely associated with the origins and history of Canada. Any birthday is an occasion for celebration. Something unusual in the way of celebration is called for on the birthday that begins the fourth century of the oldest merchandizing corporation in the world. That is what I am attempting – something unusual, a comic epic in prose. Here is a cheerful, backstairs view of three hundred years of history, enlivened by digressions, parodies, poems and other interruptions and inventions. Most of it is about the early days when the New World was new. I need claim no more for it than other advertisers do for their products, promising its readers riches, fame, and love and every other good thing. Merely to look at Mr. Searle's pictures is an infallible cure for the Vapours.

  I am, with much esteem and gratitude,
      Honourable Sirs,
       Your customer in good spirits,

        Kildare Dobbs

1

In which Medard Chouart, Sieur des
Groseilliers (known to the English as
Mister Gooseberry) & his brother-in-law,
Pierre Esprit Radisson, persuade
King Charles II of England
to
shop at the Bay

Mister Gooseberry and his brother-in-law were impressed with the greatness of England.

Every year there was something great.

First the Great Plague of 1665. Then the Great Fire of London in 1666. And in 1667, the Great Boost to shipbuilding when the Dutch sailed up the Medway and set fire to the Royal Navy.

The court was in Oxford when they arrived. They were introduced by a royal favourite who had found them in Boston, where he had been trying to explain Restoration Comedy to the Puritans.

The two renegades from New France had an Idea.

Between themselves, the Idea was to dodge tax. But they told the English Gentlemen it was a way to found colonies, make fortunes in fur, and outsmart Louis XIV, the Fun King.

Mr. Radisson did most of the talking. Everyone liked his stories.

Radisson laid it on pretty thick about the savages, as he called them.

"I love these people well!" he said, describing how they had pulled out his finger nails, chewed on his knuckles, broiled his feet. He didn't want Englishmen horning in on his territory. Not yet. He just wanted their money.

The Hon. Robert Boyle, Fellow of the Royal Society, listened attentively.

None other than the author of Boyle's Law, it was he who had demonstrated that the volume of an elastic fluid, such as air, varies inversely with the pressure. Posterity was to know him as the founder of pneumatical philosophy – and the brother of the Earl of Cork.

The Frenchmen were impressed. Especially when Boyle turned out to be a friend of the King's.

No one realized they were being asked to set up a chain of department stores.

Charles II by the Grace of God, King of England, Scotland, ffraunce and Ireland, Defender of the Faith, received the two promoters.

He was a tall king, two yards high, with black eyes, and a black wig to match. A deep crease ran down each cheek.

He played with a little spaniel while Radisson talked.

A merry monarch, he found Oxford boring. But what could he do? It was 1665, and London was rotten with the Plague. People were dying in thousands.

It was safer in Oxford. With the fellows.

Safer, but dull. These Frenchies with their adventure tales were a welcome distraction. Besides, he could practise his French.

Groseilliés & Radisson arrive in Oxford

Radisson broached the Idea.

Bypass New France to get at the Canadian fur country. The St. Lawrence river route was controlled by the three thousand French in Quebec. The Fun King's officials took too big a tax bite. Gooseberry and Radisson had found that out the hard way. That was why they had come to England with their Idea.

"There's a better route," Radisson insisted.

The English had experience of Arctic navigation. They could sail North and set up shop in Hudson Bay.

"Shop-keeping?" the King said.

"And discovery," Radisson quickly pointed out. "The Northwest Passage."

The King brightened.

These were hard times. A big spender, Parliament kept him short of cash. He had no intention of arguing with them. That was how his father Charles I had lost his head.

Luckily the Fun King kept him bankrolled, making him independent of Parliament.

Radisson was showing him new possibilities. Revenue from trade and empire might some day make him independent of the Fun King too.

He should have a note of it all.

Paper was eventually found. The Royal supplier had refused further credit. There were times when the King was short of the simplest necessities, such as clean shirts.

Three years later a hack was paid five pounds for putting Radisson's promotion literature into English.

He was a rotten speller. They were all rotten spellers. But he managed to convey the Idea, describing Radisson's voyage

> . . . *into the Great and filthy Lake of the Hurrons, Upper Sea of the East, and Bay of the North. The country was so pleasant, so beautiful & fruitfull that it grieved me to see yt. ye world could not discover such inticing countrys to live in. This I say because that the Europeans fight for a rock in the sea against one another, or for a sterrill and horrid country. . . . What conquest would that bee at litle or no cost, what laborinth of pleasure should millions of people have . . . .*

The King approved. Colonies, cash, pleasure – it was irresistible. Already there were British colonies to the south of New France. Between those and new ones to the North he could put the squeeze on the Fun King.

"Give these good fellows a chain and medal each," Charles told a courtier. "When you can find the cash."

The courtier turned up his eyes. Cash indeed.

Still, he wrote it down.

"*Chaine & medalle.*"

Years went by before the Hudson's Bay Company *paid charges in obtaining Mr. Radisson's meddall, £4.1.0.*

"Find them forty shillings a week from somewhere," the King said.

The Frenchmen bowed their thanks.

"And take them to our dear and entirely beloved cousin Rupert."

Rupert was broke. But if capital could be raised, there was profit in this Idea. Once a company was formed, it might rate a trading monopoly.

Charles was generous with such patents. Only the other day he had offered one to a man whose speciality was to stand on his head on top of church steeples.

"You don't want everyone doing that," Charles told him.

Yes, if solvent backers could be found, Charles might well grant them a charter.

'Shop-keeping?' the king said

Prince Rupert, Count Palatine of the Rhine, Duke of Bavaria and Cumberland, was conducting a chymical experiment in his Windsor Castle laboratory.

It was going badly. There must be an easier way to make money than this turning lead into gold. Might do better to stick to mezzotints. At least he had a talent for that. Courtiers couldn't very well refuse to buy.

Or sail out and capture a few Dutch prizes. Rupert enjoyed fighting. He was a reckless cavalry man, a dashing sea captain.

Too often a loser. On the field of Marston Moor he'd even lost his white poodle to that ugly Cromwell. Maybe England was unlucky for Rupert. They did not appreciate him here.

The howl they had put up during the Civil War! Just because he'd massacred a few civilians, permitted his troops a little looting and burning. Soldiers were entitled to their fun.

Why, in the Thirty Years War . . . his father, the Elector, had joined up the first week. It was still raging in Rupert's teens. He had learned a thing or two.

The alembic blew up, spattering his dressing gown.

Radisson and Gooseberry were announced.

His Highness scowled as they swept the floor with their feathered hats.

They saw a man almost as tall as the King, handsome but hard-bitten.

The Prince listened doubtfully to their sales pitch.

"Shop at the Bay, *hein*? Well, it's an idea. . . ."

He spoke good French.

"And what's this about the Northwest Passage?"

Radisson had his story ready. Here in England they were all mad about the Northwest Passage.

From the river on the Bay where they intended to trade, Radisson explained it was no more than seven days' paddling to the Stinking Lake. . . .

"Watch your stinking language!" His Highness warned. His frown deepened. "What lake is that?"

"Highness, the savages call it stink-water. In their tongue, Winnipeg."

"And this filthy river where you set up shop?"

"We could call him Rupert's river? You like?"

The Prince liked.

Radisson pursued his advantage. "From Winnipeg is not above seven days more to the strait that leads into the South Sea. And you're on your way to . . . ."

"The Spice islands! Cathay, the Empire of China!"

Rupert's eyes were shining. Northwest to Cathay! The Orient with its cloves, cinnamon, silks, opium. Unlimited china cups of tea. He showed his teeth in a smile.

"Gooseberry – you would lead this expedition?"

"If Your Highness pleases."

The Prince took a long look at this adventurer from New France. A face like an old boot. Tough and taciturn.

Rupert gripped his shoulder, gave him a shake of approval.

He turned to talkative Radisson.

"But for the present, beaver's the thing, eh?"

Radisson was glad of the chance to talk beaver. Fur would make them all rich. You bought beaver from the savages either dry or in coat.

"Coat?"

"Coats, Highness, of beaver fur, that the savages wear against the cold.'

"But if we take their coats, they'll freeze!"

"Not if we give them good woollen blankets in return . . . ."

They had just invented the Hudson Bay blanket.

Radisson went on about beaver. How the wool, or underhair, was used by felters to make hats. The best, most modish, most costly hats.

The Prince stifled a yawn.

"You must tell me about it sometime." He relented. "I did enjoy hearing about the time you were tortured. . . ."

He was afraid he could not take a very active part himself in the venture. He had decided to go to sea and give the Dutch a thrashing. A poet called Dryden said it was going to be a wonderful year. He had promised to write it up.

Rupert left the details to his secretary. James Hayes had already discussed the project with men in the City as well as with the King's ministers. He brought the Frenchmen up to date.

"In court it's the empire builders who are interested. Ashley Cooper. My Lord of Arlington. Possibly his Grace of Albemarle. . ."

Boyle and the Royal Society were eager for discoveries. The City of London merchants were just as eager for profits. And word had come from the King that he would lend a ship for the expedition.

It was March, 1669. Captain Zachariah Gillam, master of the *Nonsuch* ketch, felt the cold crackling in his hairy nostrils.

"Charles Fort. Rupert's River!" he growled. "Good job that German prince of yourn can't see it. I've a mind to strand you here when breakup comes."

"Your instructions," Mr. Gooseberry reminded him, "are to use me with all manner of civility and courtesy."

He was happy. The trade was going well, even though half the goods were missing with the *Eaglet*, the ketch lent by King Charles.

God only knew what had happened to her and Radisson after Captain Stannard had given up fighting the weather and stood for home.

He had a feeling that Radisson was all right. That fellow could talk his way out of anything. A hurricane, even.

The two men, bulky in their furs, stared at the forty-three-ton ketch, careened beside the frozen river. They stamped their feet.

Dry snow squeaked under their moccasins.

Beyond the white highway of the river the dark stand of spruce was jagged against the sky.

A sleigh-load of firewood was being hauled over the ice, dogs fanned out in front. Three small black figures followed at a stumbling trot, heads lowered against cruel wind.

"God's body but it's cold!" Gillam said.

"You call this cold, my friend?"

Nevertheless Mr. Gooseberry abruptly turned to wrench at the door of the smaller log cabin.

Gillam followed him in.

Jour instructions are to use me with all manner of civility

Icycles hung like stalactites from leaks in the roof. It was not much warmer by the stove.

Gooseberry made a suggestion.

"Use the civility to share a drop of brandy."

Gillam roared for service.

The cabin boy roused himself from his half-frozen stupor. He brought two stiff ones.

"We 'ave to go easy with this stuff, Captain," Gooseberry observed. "This is what makes us friends with the Crees."

He raised his mug.

"To our allies the Crees!"

Jean Talon, the Fun King's Intendant at Quebec, was outraged.

Now that the English had seized the Dutch posts on the Hudson River they controlled the fur trade to the South. They had made allies of the Iroquois. And the Fun King had joined fleets with them under command of James, Duke of York. Colbert, the Colonial Minister at Versailles, had warned Talon to avoid friction with them in America. For the time being, they were brothers in arms against the Dutch.

Still, business was business. One had to compete.

"I intend to compete!" Talon shouted at Governor de Courcelles.

Monsieur de Courcelles shrugged.

"It is the work of an Intendant to intend."

"Do you not understand, Governor? Those dirty Protestants are stealing our trade to the south. Now they have arrived on Hudson Bay as well!"

The Governor passed the buck.

"Speak to the Bishop."

But he had given Talon an idea.

The Bishop! The very man to help with this problem.

Talon decided to call in the Jesuits and their relations.

London, March 27, 1670. The London gentlemen gave a noisy dinner party at the Castle Tavern for the re-united explorers.

"Getting generous, they are," Captain Gillam said, chewing.

Captain Stannard was not impressed.

Gillam tried again.

"This is a bigger spread than what they give us last year at the Sun."

"The dinner at the Pope's Head last April cost near seven pound."

"This one'll cost more. You'll see."

"Beef is up."

"You know your trouble? Your trouble, me hearty, is envy. A pity you and Radisson had to turn back. Know what my cargo of beaver fetched?"

Stannard looked sour.

"Never thought to arst."

"One thousand, three hundred, and seventy-nine pound, six and four-pence."

"They lose that much at cards. The Prince and them."

Five years later Mistress Nell Gwynne, liveliest and loveliest of the King's harem, bought a bed to share with His Majesty. It had ornaments of silver, including the King's head, slaves, eagles, crowns, Cupids, and Jacob Hall dancing on a wire rope. The bill came to £1,135. 3s. 1d.

"Let not poor Nelly starve!" were Charles' last words.

London, early in 1670.

"How are we to describe this company?" the attorney asked Hayes.

"You're the solicitor."

"How about: The Governor and Mystery of . . . ."

"It's not a mystery."

"That's what the Muskovy Company calls itself."

"Pox take the Muskovy Company. And anyway, our Committee is mysterious enough."

"As you please, Sir James. What about: The Governor and Company of Merchant Adventurers of . . . ."

"No, no. Not *Merchant* Adventurers. . . ."

"But the Muskovy Company. . . ."

"Damn the Muskovites, I say!"

"We're paying good money for a copy of their charter."

"Throw it out. The Prince is *hardly* a merchant."

"Then: The Governor and Company of Gentlemen Adventurers of Eng. . . ."

"Strike out 'Gentlemen'."

The attorney slipped off his high stool. He pulled off his wig and dashed it to the floor. Then he jumped on it, three times.

"Sir, I am at a loss." He was panting. "Am I to understand, then, that the Prince is not a gentleman? That his grace of Albemarle is not a gentleman? That m'lord of Arlington is not a . . . ?"

Hudson apostrophe ess?
he observed.

"Govern your temper, sir." Sir James took a pinch of snuff. "This is a delicate matter. . . . Gentlemen do not engage in trade."

The attorney bent, groaning, to retrieve his wig.

He clapped it on his head, saying nothing. He climbed to his stool and began writing with a goose quill.

"Here!"

He handed Sir James the paper. Sir James read:

The Governor and Company of Adventurers of England
tradeing into Hudson's Bay—

"Hudson apostrophe ess?" he observed. "But let it stand. 'Tis brave. It has a singularity."

Somewhat mollified, the attorney gave a grunt.

"Now as to the territories His Majesty is conveying . . ."

"Sir, I leave that to you. I am your obedient."

Hayes bowed and left.

The territories. What was the attorney to make of the territories? Master Norwood's map was vague, to say the least. The problem was to convey land not yet discovered.

There was no question about the type of tenure.

The lands were to be held in free and common socage.

How did one pronounce that? The attorney's rage had left him confused.

In free and common sockage? Together with bootage, pantage, trouserage, and other nether garbage. Possibly with footage, leggage, hippage, waistage. Also wastage, luggage, portage, and Northwest Passage.

Or was it in free and common sausage? With porridge, spillage, spoilage, and beverage. Certainly with beaverage.

Annual rent to the Crown of two elks and two black beaver whenever the King, his heirs and successors, should set foot in the territories.

To be known as Rupert's Land.

The Adventurers to be true and absolute lords and proprietors.

Now the attorney was thoroughly confused.

"I'll begin again," he muttered.

He stared at the map.

Ridiculous names these islands had. Briggs His Mathematicks. What kind of a name was that?

Then he remembered the story. Briggs, yes. The thrice learned mathematician who had calculated from tidal drifts that there was an opening here to the west. Captain Luke Foxe had used his chart in 1631. Sighting islands where Briggs had predicted a channel, Foxe had named them for the armchair navigator.

"River beds!" the attorney suddenly exclaimed.

He had hit on the secret of Canada.

He began to scribble a draft:

Sole Trade and Commerce of all those Seas Streightes Bayes Rivers Lakes Creekes and Soundes in whatsoever Latitude they shall bee that lye within the entrance of the Streightes commonly called Hudsons Streightes together with all the Landes and Territoryes upon the Countryes Coastes . . .

When in doubt, he decided, warming to his work, give them everything.

"Odds Fish!" the King said. "I'll swear I heard a seal bark!"

Nell Gwynne made a face. It was not true that he never said a foolish thing. It was his own fault for rising so early.

Beyond the door, the Lord Privy Seal cleared his throat a second time.

"And no quips about privies!" Nell warned.

"This morning," the King said, yawning, "we are to seal the charter for the Hudson's Bay adventurers. Cousin Rupert will be waiting."

He swept the dogs off the bed with a regal gesture and began pulling on his silk stockings.

"Another day in the life of Charles the Second," he said.

"Charles the Third," Nell corrected him. Her first king, he was her third Charles.

It was May the second, 1670.

The long life of the Hudson's Bay Company was about to begin.

2

In which Governor Bayly sets up chain stores in Their Honours' Territory of Rupertsland

Shoppe at y^e Baye

"Governor of Rupert's Land," James Hayes said impressively. "'Tis a great honour!"

The Committee was meeting in the Tower of London. There was a fine view of the lawn where several queens had been beheaded.

"A great honour," Hayes repeated.

No one wanted it.

Sir John Robinson, Lieutenant of the Tower, snapped his fingers.

"I know the very man! Under this very roof, one of my prisoners!"

"Bufflehead!" Hayes growled. "We've adventured money. Shall we trust it to a jailbird?"

"I'll warrant he's honest! One that grew up in the King's bosom, but a Quaker!"

Quakers were notoriously honest. All England was in uproar with their message of love. The prisons were full of them.

"What else is there to commend him?"

"He's bilingual."

"Bring him in!"

"Let me out of here," Bayly said. "That's all."

"Are you not the fellow that foretold the plague and the fire?" a Committee member asked the prisoner.

"I sent a few words in love and kindness to the King, warning him of God's Wrath."

"Treason!"

"Nay, I spoke tenderly. I did but rebuke his rioting and excess of drinking and playing, his great chambering and wantonness." The prisoner sighed. "Today I care naught for such things. I live in love toward all. I am beyond all strife and contention."

"Will you take the oath of allegiance if we let you out?"

"No. What does it matter? I love the King. We were boys together at his father's court."

The goldsmith Portman narrowed his eyes.

"What other jails have you been in?"

Bayly lifted his chin. There was something noble about him, perhaps his eyes. With his long white beard he looked an old man. Suffering had marked him.

"Friend, I have been in all the best dungeons in Europe."

No. Nor go to the idol-house neither...

1670. Outward bound for the Bay, the *Prince Rupert* was a sail on the horizon. High on the poop-deck of the good ship *Wivenhoe*, Captain Newland bellowed commands at his crew.

"Unshackle the spantle! Belay the larboard stashing-strake! Roundly there, me 'earties! Smack it about a bit!"

Radisson was spliced to the main brace.

Governor Bayly had lashed himself to a convenient marline-spike with a bowline on a bight, two round turns and a half-hitch, a double Matthew Walker, and a granny-knot.

The *Wivenhoe* yawed. A monstrous green breaker crashed over the stern.

Captain Newland bellowed some more.

"Clear fog-lockers, you poxy jumped-up oars' gets! On oilskins! Stow the starboard warps, button the flies, and cooks to the galley! And don't dilly-dally! Hands to bends and hitches and mend their britches! Lay aft handsomely, you rotten, tired sea-daddies!"

"These English," Radisson said, bored. "I'll tell you the story of my adventures."

"No," Bayly decided. "I'll tell thee mine."

He was, after all, the Governor.

Bayly was twelve or thirteen when his troubles began. The Civil War broke out. Officers at the court of Charles I and his French queen were dismissed, Bayly's French parents among them.

They fled to France. Their son followed later with the French ambassador for whom he'd been interpreter. But he had been infected with dangerous notions. Something in him, he insisted, could not be satisfied to feed at the tables of princes. He ran away from home and returned to England. At Gravesend he met a man called Bradstreet, a 'spirit' who enticed him on board ship. Sold as a bond-slave, he spent seven years of servitude in 'Maryland, Virginia'.

"It was a time of hunger, cold, and nakedness," he recalled. "Many times was I stripped naked and tied up by the hand and whipped. And made to go barefoot and bare-legged in cold and frosty weather and hardly clothes to cover my nakedness. I ate bread in the ash-heap – "

"You call this 'ardship?"

"Instead of a well-strung lute in my hand, I had hard labour. And I vowed I should be a true and faithful witness against the spirit of persecution, murder, and envy in whomsoever it be!"

"You became a heretic!"

"A friend. Elizabeth Harris gave me the message. The spirit came on me. All I wanted was to tell people to repent and love one another. This . . . this feeling would come over me, and before I knew it I was giving forth – like the time I spoke to the merchants of London."

"What did you say?"

" 'O thou inhabitants and city of London,' I said. 'O the desolation which is coming upon you,' I said. 'O ye Babylonish merchants! Weeping and woeful lamentation is coming upon you, and all the inhabitants of the earth shall hate, utterly loathe, and abominate your merchandize!' That's the sort of stuff I said back in 1663."

"*Ciel!* I 'ope you were wrong this time!"

"I hope so too."

The *Wivenhoe*'s fat womb was crammed with London trade-goods for sale to the Indians.

Freed, Bayly had returned to Europe. In Rome he spoke lovingly to the Pope. The Inquisition, disapproving, threw Bayly into the city Bedlam. In straw and chains he went on hunger strike till they let him go, banishing him forever on pain of perpetual galley-slavery.

From this moment, whenever he caught sight of a parson, Bayly could not help accosting him with kindly words. The habit cost him months in French prisons. And in England once more, in the streets of Bristol, he was unlucky enough to run into two gentlemen of the cloth.

He was thrown into Newgate jail.

Charles liked Quakers. When William Penn came before him and failed to remove his hat, Charles uncovered his own head. Penn wanted to know why. "'Tis the custom in this place," the King said, smiling, "that when two are together, one of them uncovers."

Charles had Bayly removed to the Tower, the most comfortable prison in the kingdom.

Bayly—in prison as usual

Governor Bayly nailed the King's Arms to a tree at Port Nelson in the mouth of the Nelson River. There were no Indians to trade with but it was a nice place. Or was till storms blew the ship out to sea and the men started going sick and dying.

Mr. Gooseberry had gone on in the *Prince Rupert* to Charles Fort. Discouraged, Bayly decided to abandon the new post and join him.

The brief, sweltering summer with its clouds of mosquitoes and black-flies was followed by the frightful cold of winter.

Bayly shuddered. Maryland had not been like this.

" 'The country so pleasant,' eh, Radisson? 'So beautiful and fruitful' – wasn't that it?"

Radisson shifted uneasily.

"There's always the trade. I could open a branch in Moose River. . . ."

"Do." Bayly sighed. "I'll call for volunteers to settle here. We'll kill one of the pigs."

The men enjoyed their roast pork. No one volunteered.

"Stop here!" Father Albanel, s.j., told his paddling Indians.

They beached and hid the canoe.

It was June of 1672. The Jesuit and his relations – Sebastian Pennara and Paul Denis, Sieur de Saint Simon – had arrived overland from New France.

Charles Fort could not be far away now. They had seen a savage wrapped in a new Hudson's Bay Company blanket.

Albanel hesitated. It was the custom of Jesuits to disguise themselves. One hated to arrive sacerdotally naked. Should he change costumes with one of his savages? The black cassock he wore over his furs was very conspicuous.

On the other hand, if he arrived in disguise, everyone would know at once that he was a Jesuit.

Whereas if he wore the black robe openly no one would believe he could possibly be what he was. Yes, the double bluff. That was the thing. One had to keep up the reputation of one's order.

He laughed subtly, a little wizened old man bundled in black.

They met more and more Indians in Hudson's Bay Company blankets.

father Albanel reaches Charles Fort

Ronald Searle

For a moment, the Jesuit toyed with the notion of wearing one himself. No, it was too obvious. Instead, he absent-mindedly baptised the Indians as he went, not forgetting to warn them that trading with dirty English Protestants was displeasing to the Fun King and his servant the Bishop.

And now they were in sight of the Bay post, a snug settlement high on the left bank of the river. The Jesuit halted. Something was wrong. There was no ship beached on the foreshore. No smoke coming from the fort's chimneys.

He smiled with holy cunning. No ship, *hein*? No smoke, *hein*? Oh, it was clever all right, but they wouldn't catch a seasoned traveller like himself that way. It was a trap, of course.

It took Albanel about an hour to adjust to the notion that this was no ambush, that the fort had simply been abandoned. Then he cheered up.

"We three Frenchmen with only eight Indians have captured this English Fort!"

He nailed the Fun King's Arms to the Bay Store. Then, after baptising the remaining Indians, he settled down to bargain for their furs.

It was a pleasure to do business with Christians.

English ships, though, could reach the Bay more easily than Jesuits. By late summer Bayly was back, and doing so well from his factories at Charles Fort, Moose River, Albany, and sales trips up the coast, that the Adventurers back in London were convinced he must be cheating them.

The Charter laid down the rules. The name of the game was Monopoly. The Committee sat around a table in the Royal Mint and played it by coal and candle light.

Spies had told them Bayly made no use of the books of Common Prayer they had sent out. A man so free in his thinking must be free in his trading as well. It looked as if he had already misapplied £828. 15s. 6d. They were nursing an interloper. And paying him all of fifty pounds a year.

Private enterprise – they'd soon put a stop to that. Quaker indeed. The fellow was no better than an Anabaptist.

Lydall. "No rationing. We'll starve together if necessary"

September 15, 1674.

Charles Fort, Rupert River.

Food was running out. If relief did not arrive within the next two days, Bayly decided, everyone in the fort would have to set sail for England in the only ship they had – the little *Employ*.

The Jesuit was with them. This time Albanel had brought a letter for Mr. Gooseberry. It was from Frontenac, the new French Intendant.

Bayly would have liked to know what was in it. He suspected, correctly, that the Fun King was trying to tempt the Frenchmen back into his service. It was to forestall this that one of the Adventurers had persuaded Radisson to marry his daughter. But Mr. Gooseberry was immune to such ties. He already had a wife. Still, Governor Bayly was worried.

Not that the Jesuit bothered him. He had, after all, been called a Jesuit himself. Apart from a few seasonable observations, spoken in loving plainness, to the effect that all idols, all idolatries, and idol priests must perish, Bayly had treated Albanel kindly.

"Men fall a-quarrelling and killing one another about the apostles' words," Bayly remarked. "This is not the nature of Christians."

The Jesuit tightened his lips. No one could be so simple-hearted as this heretic appeared.

Two days later the *Rupert*, under Gillam's command, and the *Shaftesbury* stood into the river.

Bayly was overjoyed.

Not for long. William Lydall had arrived to relieve him as Governor. Bayly was to return to England to face charges of private trading.

Bayly handed over to Lydall without argument. But it was now too late in the season for his voyage home. They settled in together for the winter, a cosy, strictly-rationed party. The new Governor and the ex-Governor; the Quaker and the Jesuit; the disaffected Mr. Gooseberry and the Englishmen.

They gave the new Governor a hard time. So hard Lydall decided to quit when Spring dissolved the ice in 1675.

Charles Bayly was Governor again. Three years later the Committee raised his salary to £200 and sent out his viol so that he could make music in the wilderness.

On his return to England, Mr. Gooseberry had joined Radisson and immediately defected with him to the Fun King.

Dark days were ahead for the Company. But Bayly, tranquilly fiddling beside the sea, had set up an impressive chain of stores. The Indians, despite French attempts to dissuade them, were beginning to make a habit of shopping at the Bay.

3

Of the Trade and its Circumstances

PRO PELLE CUTEM

The Shield! The Canadian Shield!

Come, Muse of rockbound nationalists, for whom our stammering typing engine waits smiling with teeth of alphabets. You who inflate the eloquence of Northern laureates, come, let us celebrate the real estate. Sing, learned dame – as so often before – not of men, not of poor flesh and blood, but of rocks, stones, mud, bogs, fens, muskegs, permafrost, tundra!

The Shield. Some of it was gneiss. But mostly it was nearly two million square miles of acid rocks. Tell it, Muse, pneumatically, puffed up with more than heroic simile.

Like some unimaginably vast dragon coiled with armoured tail in frigid Labrador and monstrous head raised in jagged cordilleras of the Arctic northwest, it had groaned under the crushing burden of three waves of glaciers far back in geological time. Then, as when ponderous with platitudes the leaden-mouthed speaker bores and depresses the sated dinner guest; so, heavy with adjectives, the implacable glaciers had crunched and clawed at its igneous, ignominious old rocks.

So immense was this saurian with scales of adamant, stretching through time zones, that when dawn with boozy fingers was plucking at its tail, evening was already thickening the air about its rocky head!

As late as the Upper Plastocine the Canadian Shield was unwanted. It was dismissed as Precambrian.

By the time man had arrived in the vain hope of finding better country than Siberia, it was useless for farming. Most of it, in fact, was covered with forest.

"Boreal, that's what it is," the men said yawning.

Luckily the Shield was swarming with animals in fur coats.

And lakes, myriads of them brimming with cold water. Company men used it to dilute their good spirits. A hundred and ninety gallons of brandy; twelve gallons of French brandy; ten gallons and two quarts of usquebaugh or Irish whiskey – it was barely enough to keep one trading-post in good spirits for one winter. Yet they had been in good spirits since 1670.

That was why the Indians came to see them.

Through the lakes of the Shield and their connecting rivers, the Indians moved swiftly in birchbark canoes. Came freeze-up, they travelled on racquets or dog sleds.

Before the white men came they had not been able to travel much. They had had to live beside their kettles which, being made from hollow logs, were too heavy to move. Filled with water, which their owners boiled by throwing in hot stones, they were heavier still.

Once the Indians got portable copper kettles from the traders, they were free to go on sales trips. They set up in business for themselves.

the savages moved swiftly .. business was business

Not yet a department store
— but they were getting there

No one could understand why the palefaces came all the way across the ocean in small, expensive sailing-ships to beg for old, greasy beaver coats.

Still, business was business.

Indians did not believe in private property. They believed in public ownership and collective bargaining. The English called them Red Indians.

But they still had a sweet deal going for them. They passed off their old clothes on the crazy palefaces. Then, having worn out the incredibly precious goods they got in exchange, they passed these off on the tribes of the interior: blunt knives, broken kettles, and awls in return for prime furs.

For money they used beaver skins. There was no haggling over prices, which were fixed in terms of beaver by the Standard of Trade. This was arrived at by treaty, pledged in firewater, tobacco smoke, and strings of coloured beads, used as memoranda, called wampum.

The Company palefaces did not speak with two tongues. The motto of the Governor and Company of Adventurers of England was *Pro pelle cutem*. Which, being loosely interpreted, signifies: Skin me, cutey, and I'll skin you.

Factories, the stores were called. It took off the taint of retail. By 1682 there were three of them at the south end of James Bay (known, ominously, as the Bottom of the Bay): Rupert's House, Moose Factory and Albany Factory. A fourth, York Factory, had been built at the mouth of the Hayes and Nelson Rivers.

The men in charge were called factors.

To most factors and their men the interior remained a vast and hostile mystery. Yet it was all part of the territory Charles II had bestowed on them. And now the Fun King wanted it.

England and France were contending for the Canadian Shield. Whoever won it three times running would get to keep it.

Bitter trouble was ahead for the factories. The upper country held no terrors for the French, who had gone native. Already Radisson, now on their side, had seized one of the factories. They were armed with cannon and fortified with bastions, palisades, and redoubts. But this was barely enough to protect them against customers during sales. It could not be expected to keep out the competition.

Yet as long as they could, the Indians shopped at the Bay.

We love the English ...

Here they could buy the finest English manufactures. Baize, bayonets, and beads; bells, blankets, brandy, and burning glasses; buttons, chisels, cloth, and combs; cottons, duffel, eardrops; feathers, files, flannel, and flints; gartering, glasses, gunpowder, guns; hatchets, hats, horns (powder); kettles, knives, lace, pots, rings, runlets; sashes, shirts, shoes, shot, and stockings; thread, tobacco, trunks, and twine; vermilion; red and white waters. The brandy was inferior to the French product. In reality it was a kind of gin. But it was better than lake-water.

Not yet a department-store chain. But they were getting there.

It was easy to spot the leader, splendid in his scarlet coat and cocked hat. The other Indians wore blankets or beaver-robes.

"Wotcher, cock!" the factor said, reading from his phrase book. He corrected himself. "I mean *watcheer coshock!* How do you, friend?"

"Thank you. How do you?"

Neither answered this question. The topic was too depressing. Each made a habit of catching the other's diseases. The Indians caught smallpox or measles and died of them. The English got scurvy and at first their mortality, too, was high. They kept getting ruptured. Sometimes they came down with the Iliac Passion.

When they suffered frostbite the Company surgeon was on hand to trim off toes, noses, etc. The very first voyage under the Charter had been tended by Peter Romulus, ye French chirurgion. Despite the rule of *economy in all things*, Their Honours issued cases of instruments.

The leader held out a grimy hand for the factor's pipe.

"Let me smoke with you, friend!"

He took a puff. His dark features creased in a grimace.

"This tobacco has a bad taste – I will not trade it."

The best Brazil! But the factor remembered his instructions *You are to treat the Natives with the utmost Civility and Kindness.*

"I'll open another. Will you trade today?"

"Tomorrow. But we'll trade some brandy now. The young men want to drink."

Back in the fort, the factor did not forget to lock the door behind him. *Natives not to be suffer'd to come into the Trading, or taught to write or Read or otherwise admitted to prye into any of the Company's affairs.* At least one unlucky child had evaded this rule. He had learned enough to write to the Committee, begging to be brought to London and baptised. Their Honours were appalled.

The factor passed out brandy at the trading window.

"Make haste – it will be night! And you'll be drunk in the morning and not trade."

"Ho, ho," the Indians said.

They had come hundreds of miles for this brandy.

Heads aching, the Indians were admitted to the fort for the Trading Ceremony.

It was a solemn ritual, the leader tricked out in his fanciest duds.

He and the factor sat on chairs and smoked together the *calamity*, or piece of pipe. At intervals they waved it importantly, pointing the mouthpiece to every quarter of the compass. Then it was passed from hand to hand till the whole, silent company had had a go.

Flowery speeches were made. But not so flowery that the leader failed to make his point. Prices were fixed at the agreed standard. What the Indians were concerned about was quality.

"Here is a great many young men come with me. Use them kindly I say! Give them good goods, give them good goods I say!" He began to scold. "We lived hard last winter, and in want. The powder being in short measure and bad I say! Tell your servants to fill the measure and not to put their fingers within the brim. Take pity of us, take pity of us I say!"

The factor listened intently. The customer was often right.

"We come a long way to see you," the leader insisted. "The French sends for us but we will not hear. We love the English."

"Ho," the Indians said.

An old man began a dramatic harangue about the tribal enemies.

"They come and kill us. We don't want to kill them but they're always coming against us! What do you say to it?"

The way the factor saw it, it did not make much difference what he said. His customers would choose the warpath anyway. London kept pestering him to make peace among the tribes. It was the right thing to do – and also good for trade. For form's sake, he made some soothing remarks.

They went down badly. To the Indians, a trade treaty was an alliance. They expected their paleface brothers to help in their wars. The Fun King's men understood this better than the English.

And every year the cargoes of fur arrived in London.

At a Committee meeting on September 29, 1682, a warehouse-keeper was hired for thirty pounds a year. He was to be bonded in the amount of one thousand pounds.

Three gentlemen were deputed to view possible warehouses.

"*To lodg the beavor*," the secretary noted.

The chairman was drawing rings on his blotter.

"Why not?" he muttered. "A circular church like the Holy Sepulchre! Oh, I knew they'd never let me do it. The canons so backward . . ."

"What? What?" Mr. Craddock said. "Designing St. Paul's again?"

Sir Christopher Wren looked up guiltily.

"It could have been the biggest dome ever built. But the canons . . ."

Sir Christopher Wren

"And on our time!" Mr. Craddock pointed out. "Why not do something for us on the dean's and chapter's time?"

"Compromises. Always compromises," the architect muttered.

"You might design us decent locks and bolts for the new warehouse."

"Seconded!" Mr. Weymans said quickly.

The motion was carried unanimously.

The Secretary wrote: '*Ordered that such Shutters, bolts and locks, be made to the warehouse as Sr. Chris. Wren shall judg fitt to be done . . .*'

He looked up. Sir Christopher was drawing rings again, sighing and shaking his head. It was obvious he had already forgotten the whole arrangement.

The secretary pursed his lips. He made another note.

"*And the Secretary to see it accordingly done with Expedition.*"

Not that Their Honours were pacifists. The early Governors were warlike enough. When Rupert died, he was succeeded by the Duke of York, another military and naval commander.

The Duke lost his position when he followed his brother on the throne as James II. He never could hold down a job. He lost his crown to his daughter Mary and her husband William the Orangeman.

The new Governor, John Churchill, later Duke of Marlborough, was to become the toughest of English generals.

Son of Sir Winston, a solid knight in the Commons, Churchill had a hard head for business. History's highest-paid gigolo, his first five thousand was a gift from Barbara, Duchess of Cleveland, one of Charles' mistresses.

She had got ten thousand pounds from Sir Edward Hungerford for one night, and given half to Churchill. The King caught Churchill with her. "I forgive you, sir," he sneered, "for I know you do but earn your bread."

Gossip has it that, later on, when Barbara was short of gambling money, Marlborough coldly refused her request for a loan. The Duchess burst her stays with vexation. Alexander Pope remembered her as the fair one.

Who of ten thousand gulled her Knight,
Then asked ten thousand for another night.
The gallant, too, to whom she paid it down,
Lived to refuse his mistress half-a-crown.

4

In which Sieurs, Wood Runners,
Voyageurs, Jesuits & other French
Competitors harass the
Honourable Company
until
at last defeated upon the Plains
of Abraham

PRO PELLE CUTEM

Pierre LeMoyne, Sieur d'Iberville, also known as the Canadian Cid, arrived at Moose Fort by canoe one night in 1686. With him were two of his ten brothers, a Jesuit, and four-score French soldiers under command of the Chevalier de Troyes. They had travelled overland from Montreal.

Not that they were at war with the English. This was business.

There were two kinds of business competition. The bourgeois kind was a matter of cutting prices and giving service. The noble kind was rougher. The LeMoyne boys were noble.

Ignoring the ornamental cannon on the redoubts, they attacked at dawn, bashing in the blockhouse door with a tree-trunk.

The Canadian Cid charged through the opening – and everything went black. *Ciel*, he was blinded!

Mais non, the door has slammed behind him . . . The flash of his pistol-shot gave a glimpse of figures milling about in their shirts. He hacked about him in the dark, reckless in the certainty that anything he cut belonged to heretics. And if he himself was hurt, there were plenty more LeMoynes where this one came from.

Half-an-hour later the Company men, still in their good-quality shirts, had called it quits.

Removing two small cannon as souvenirs, the Cid and his brothers set off under de Troyes for Rupert's House.

They found the *Craven* moored below the post. The Cid took two canoes to capture her. A man wrapped in a Company blanket on deck resisted and was shot. The other hands were snoring below. The Cid had to stamp on deck to wake them.

The storming of the fort began at first light with a ghastly racket of musketry and cannon and grenades thrown down chimneys. A wounded English lady, companion to the Governor's wife (who happened to be with her husband at Albany), was first to surrender.

The Cid took her on board the *Craven* for the trip to Albany, anchoring discreetly in the river's mouth.

De Troyes and his troops approached the fort the hard way. Exhausted by the long march overland, his men struggled to dig in the cannon as he demanded the English surrender.

He was bluffing. The fort bristled with cannon – forty-three of them. His men were too starved to fight.

Fight? Governor Sergeant had no intention of it. Not with ladies present. Let the French fire a few shots by way of excuse and he'd come to terms.

He was at supper with his wife and chaplain when de Troyes obliged. A servant was pouring wine as the first cannon-ball whizzed past Mrs. Sergeant's nose and the second under his own arm. Mrs. Sergeant fainted.

The English quickly surrendered (to the French)

Next morning, first piously attending mass, the Frenchmen began a fierce bombardment.

They got up enough strength to shout, "*Vive le roy!*"

That did it. Trembling in his cellar, the Governor sent out the parson with a white flag. Soon he surrendered with much pompous fuss and offers of wine.

De Troyes tried to hurry things along. Surely the heretics would notice the state of his men! But Sergeant had had a bad fright and his conditions were easy. De Troyes quickly accepted.

Leaving d'Iberville in command, he returned to Montreal.

The Canadian Cid broke the agreement almost at once. He never kept a promise unless he had to. Ever the noble competitor, he crammed his prisoners into a yacht to make their way to the Company post at Port Nelson.

Rations were short till twenty men died, *frozen and Starved and some faine to bee Eaten up by the Rest of the Company.*

The Bottom of the Bay was now in French hands. The Company was out by some £50,000. Only York Factory and Port Nelson remained.

In addition to the factories there was one other asset. Radisson had changed sides again in 1684 and was back with the Company.

For the London gentlemen these were trying times. Suing the chicken-hearted Governor on his return for £20,000, they ended by having to pay him £350.

The Canadian Cid was still the scourge of the Bay.

By 1689, England and France now formally at war, the Cid had captured a sloop, a shallop, and three ships, all Company property. Peace or war, he fought brilliantly and he fought dirty.

The same year two Company ships, outward bound, got no farther than the Channel. A French privateer captured one and sent the other limping back to Plymouth.

Even at home the Company had enemies. They published nasty things. A Diminutive Company, they said. With an unprecedented boundless Charter, they said. And forts no better than pig-styes, they said.

The Committee became more secretive than ever, even paranoid.

They had always been jealous of their best servants. In the early days there had been the case of one William Bond. *Put himself out of the Company service by over valueing himselfe,* they noted. And now, in 1687, a year of great danger, they let James Knight go.

They suspected him of private enterprise. He was, after all, a Yankee.

He had joined as a carpenter eleven years earlier, had built the houses at Moose and Albany, worked as shipwright, given good advice on policy and outfitting. Promoted Deputy Governor to Nixon, he had stayed on to see the cowardly Sergeant put over his head. Now he was let go.

But Knight could take care of himself. By 1682, when the Committee begged him to return as Governor and Commander of the Bottom of the Bay, he was rich enough to make his own terms.

The same year, from his base at York Factory, he took three ships to winter on the Eastmain in readiness for an attack on Albany.

The assault went in on July 2, 1693. Two of Knight's men were killed and several wounded before the French suddenly ceased fire.

The quiet was uncanny. Maybe it was a trap.

Yet there was no ambush when the English burst into the fort. Flies buzzed in the silence. The garrison had taken to the woods – all five of them.

From one of the deserted buildings, the invaders heard sounds. Some-one was moaning and gibbering in there.

It was the fort armourer. He was already in chains. He had gone raving mad and murdered a Jesuit and a surgeon before being over-powered.

More gratifying than the crazy prisoner were the thirty-one thousand beaver skins.

The loss of the James Bay posts was a blow to the Canadian Cid. He realized their importance to the trade. He had tried the river route into the fur country. The Bay route was better.

Absent from Hudson Bay the season of Knight's victory, he returned next year to compete. With two borrowed royal ships and the inevitable Jesuit, the Cid swooped on York Factory. The English, short of firewood, were soon frozen out.

The Cid turned his shivering prisoners into the woods to fend for themselves. They had a wretched winter. Even the victors suffered; snug in the fort, some twenty died of scurvy.

But d'Iberville netted the Company's stock of forty-five thousand beaver.

Leaving the priest and a garrison, he sailed for France.

The Committee had at last got the hang of noble competition.

In 1696 they sent three of their ships with two men-o'-war to recapture York Factory.

It was a boozy voyage, with eighteen casks of brandy to keep the naval men in good spirits. Despite the damage to livers, the expedition was a success. York was recovered after a siege.

Borrowing the d'Iberville technique, the English played dirty. They reneged on the terms of surrender and seized the French hoard of beaver – almost thirty thousand skins.

And back in the Old World, William the Orangeman and the Fun King agreed to stop fighting for a while. By the Treaty of Ryswick, signed in September, 1697, everything was to be put back the way it was before the war. The Company would have to hand over all posts.

Luckily no one in Hudson Bay knew it. Least of all d'Iberville.

In July he was standing into Hudson Strait with a flotilla of five sail, himself in the *Pelican*.

Two of his force had been damaged in collision, the crews were riddled with scurvy, and a third ship had foundered in the ice. Late in August the Cid lost touch with his three consorts in heavy fog.

Arriving off York Factory, he anchored and waited for them. He sent a party ashore to reconnoitre the fort.

Next day the lookout reported three sail on the horizon.

The missing ships! thought d'Iberville, pleased.

His face changed as he squinted through his telescope.

Species of pigs! These were no Frenchmen. They were English!

"Drummer!" he hollered. "Beat to quarters!"

Weighing anchor, he took another look. They were coming on in line ahead, led by the *Hampshire*, a warship of fifty-two guns. And in her wake the Company ships *Dering* (thirty guns) and *Hudson's Bay* (thirty-two guns).

The Cid had forty-five guns. With men ashore and forty other in the sickbay, he was outgunned and undermanned.

But he was the Cid. Therefore the odds were in his favour. He ran head on at the *Hampshire*, forcing her to luff clear.

Next, he gave the *Dering* a blast of grape to tickle her tackle. The rest of his broadside picked the teeth of the *Hudson's Bay*.

Never had the icy waters of the Bay witnessed such a battle. The wind puffed, the ships luffed; spray flew, the gale blew; the ships wore, the men swore; the ships tacked, muskets cracked, gunners sweated and toiled, guns banged, clouds of smoke boiled and rolled over the severely agitated waves. Shot screamed and rattled in sheets and ratlines, rigging ravelled, booms boomeranged, yards splintered, timbers cracked and split, sailors broke in two or came apart at the seams, blood ran rivering over the nice scrubbed decks. From tumbling masts and spars, wrecked and ruined by whizzing hotshots, seabirds flew squawking to dip in the foaming wake for severed limbs and other bits and pieces.

And on board the embattled *Hampshire*, Captain Fletcher R.N., trying to work up to windward for the weather gage, found the Cid sailing abreast of him. Gad, if he had to be killed, he was going to get smashed first! This called for a drink.

The Canadian Cid had the same thought.

Grinning like sea-wolves, they drank to each other.

Their two broadsides crashed like exploding volcanoes.

It was good night for Captain Fletcher. Moments later his ship was sinking with all hands – 290 men.

The Cid stared at his glass. *Formidable!* He had not known this stuff was so good.

Then back to capture the *Hudson's Bay*! The *Dering* escaped.

A gale blew up that night, wrecking the *Hudson's Bay* and drowning most of her 190 crew.

The *Pelican*, too, went aground. The Cid had been unseamanlike enough to anchor off a lee shore. But he got most of his men and gear safely to land.

His three missing ships came up as he made ready to take the fort.

The furs he won were valued at £20,000.

Gloom descended on the coffee houses where Their Honours did business. What had happened to the rules of Monopoly? With all this noble competition there was no longer much percentage in beaver. Captured furs, though costed at nil, only helped glut the market.

They were put up for auction by the candle. Even though the Company laid on three dozen each of sack and claret, the action was sluggish.

Sale by the candle was meant to be exciting. True, buyers traditionally hung back at the start, when the auctioneer lit his inch of candle. But once the flame began to gutter, they were supposed to yell their bids and keep yelling. Last bid before the flame died – the winner! Yet now, even at that critical moment when the smoke dipped just before the end, there was hardly a murmur.

There was no fun in a buyers' market.

The Committee were strapped. To their Plymouth agent they confessed: "*Wee are verry much streitened for Pecunia.*"

That was in 1695. For five years there had been no dividend. There would not be another till 1718.

Twenty-eight years without a dividend!

The Adventurers were distracted, busy with new-fangled inventions.

London was evolving the National Debt, the Bank of England, the Stock Exchange, not to speak of Whigs, Tories, and Public Works. Wren was building all over the place. Rebellion, crime, Popery were rampant. The biggest war since the Crusades had broken out in 1702 – eight million British islanders with all the allies they could buy against nineteen million French. Department stores would have to wait.

Twenty-eight years was a long time. But Their Honours were nothing if not patient. They slurped their dishes of tea and waited.

Certain things were going their way. Among Protestant refugees from France were most of the skilled hatters of Paris. They were making London the Hat Capital of the World – promising a strong market for beaver felt.

On the Continent, Marlborough, though no longer with the Company was clobbering the competition at Blenheim, Malplaquet, and other tourist centres.

And silently, almost without knowing it, British ships and sailors had taken command of the seas. Hearts of oak had snatched and held Gibraltar, Newfoundland, Nova Scotia.

The great thing was to win the treaties. The Peace of Utrecht, 1713, gave back all Hudson Bay to England and the Adventurers.

From now on if anyone was to win by playing dirty it was not going to be the French.

Henceforth none but Britannia waived the rules.

"A bargain is a bargain," as James Knight put it, taking over York Factory, "so long as it is not to the Company's loss."

To the old man, now in his seventies, it did not look much of a bargain. The Frenchies had left a mess behind them; the fort all rotten and ready to fall, the gun-carriages disintegrating. Knight's own quarters were not half so good as his old cowhouse at Albany.

The ex-carpenter did not repine. He could always build.

He grumbled about his men. Though all were names and eaters, not all were workers. But he soon got the place snug and ship-shape.

He was tough. He stood for no nonsense from London, himself a Committee member and stockholder of twelve years standing.

"It cannot be thought," he warned them, "that you that are at that distance can see or know altogether how things goes here so well as I do that am upon the Spott . . . There is no Man fitt to Serve you, that must be told his Business."

The Committee was at last in professional hands. City hands – no more socialites or academics. In charge was Sir Bibye Lake. He was lucky. The South Sea Bubble burst before he could blow capital into it. A friend had warned: "That bubble's trouble, Bibye, baby!" He knew when to take a hint. He was durable, the Perpetual Governor. Knight and he understood one another.

Knight's policy was to let the customers do the walking. It was more thrifty than to set up posts inland. He and his men were sailors. They did not care to go far from the sea. The Bay was theirs. Why venture into the stony bosom of the Shield, a region still in dispute? It was enough to send out an occasional traveller to drum up sales, especially to the northward.

Not that Knight was content to sit still. His old eyes glittered with dreams of whale fisheries, copper, gold.

The French had lost the Bay but they still swarmed in the Shield. They began a campaign that mixed bourgeois and noble competition.

The bourgeois part consisted in offering premiums and home delivery. As premium, they had a winner in French brandy. The Indians found it a bewitching liquor.

For home delivery the French relied on two kinds of colonists – pedlars and paddlers.

The pedlars were *coureurs de bois* or wood runners (not to be confused with the wooden Indians who advertised tobacco). They ran through the woods to make deliveries right at the customer's wigwam or tepee. Shod for the heavy winter snows, they were raqueteers.

The paddlers were a special breed of Canadian. They had developed immense chest and arm muscles from paddling the big birchbark canoes of furs and trade goods to and from Montreal. As fuel, they burnt tobacco; they smoked incessantly, measuring distances in pipefuls. They were called *voyageurs* and their most deadly weapon was song. The breakers of Long Sault curled in terror, Niagara roared with pain at the fearsome raucous racket of their *En roulant ma boule boulant*. Indians stuffed moss and clay in their ears, wild beasts fled in terror, trees split and dropped their needles, rocks were shattered!

These were the heroes who followed La Vérendrye and his sons into the West.

Pierre Gaultier de Varennes, Sieur de la Vérendrye, was, of course, noble, and he meant to compete for the Hudson's Bay trade by noble means.

He began to move West and North along the river routes, always with that terrible music in his ears, building forts as he went. The Indians responded well to home delivery and good cognac, but where these bourgeois persuasions failed, muscle had to be used. The Sieur's sons and wood runners fanned out from the strong points to intercept and menace the fleets of customers on their way to shop at the Bay.

La Vérendrye had been wounded and taken prisoner at Malplaquet by Marlborough's victorious troops. Here in the wild wastes of the Shield he could get back at the Company, dinting their dividends. He taught his paddlers to sing *Malbrouck s'en va t'en guerre*.

He moved slowly. At Kaministikwia (now Fort William), Rainy Lake, Lake of the Woods, Lake Winnipeg, one by one his fortified posts went up. It was 1738 before he built one at the forks of the Red and Assiniboine Rivers. Much later it was named for the Stinking Lake – Winnipeg.

September, 1759. It was a bore squatting on the edge of the St. Lawrence, staring across the wide waters at Quebec.

Montcalm and his men were probably laughing, sitting tight in the Château Frontenac behind thick walls. Guarded by the river and its high-cliffed shoreline.

Wolfe, the British general, seemed to have no fixed plan. He spent much time pondering in the latrine.

Next thing they were in the boats, the waters around them black in the smothering darkness. It was chilly. The Fraser Highlanders wound on their mufflers, as ordered.

"On the *oars*, you fools!" the General hissed.

A line of poetry came into his mind. *The paths of glory lead but to the grave*. Gray's *Elegy*. I'd rather write that than follow it, he thought. Poets were lucky dogs.

Somehow they were up the cliff without being spotted, and onto the Plains of Abraham in front of the city walls.

Bugles sang as the thin red line dressed. Puffing with exertion, Wolfe straightened up, pulled in his non-existent chin and surveyed the field.

The French were coming out to fight, advancing in a great heap, yelling and firing. The redcoats waited, motionless.

At last their volley crashed out.

All was smoke, confusion, noise.

Indian war whoops from skirmishers on the flanks, screams of wounded, clan war cries from the bloodthirsty Highlanders, French oaths, shots, clash of steel, bugle calls.

Wolfe was surprised to find himself lying on the ground, supported by one of his officers.

Someone was singing a nursery rhyme.

See how they run,

See how they run . . .

How confusing it was! It all seemed so far off now.

"Who run?"

"Why, sir, the French!" a voice seemed to be saying.

Wolfe smiled. The light was fading. Three blind mice . . . Yes, yes. Would much rather have written that than . . .

And in a house, inside the fallen city where his men had carried him, the Marquis de Montcalm too was dying.

So he had lost Quebec. Well, he had never liked the place anyway. Luckily he would not be here long.

The nuns nursing him were pretty. Montcalm could lose his head to these ladies.

They kept it in a glass box for more than two hundred years.

The Royal Navy arrived in time to prevent the recapture of Quebec.

The British had won the Canadian Shield and meant to keep it.

5.

In which is offered a Riddling Bestiary, or Sequence of Beastly Riddles, being an introduction to the fur-bearing Creatures; together with Notes and a Dissertation on the Beaver.

Pacing the margins of a floe,
To and fro, to and fro
I walk my rage
As in a cage
And sometimes eat an Eskimo.

Warm in my robe of horrid white,
I walk my rage all winter's night.
Fair game am I for cunning men
Whose fat I chew on now and then.

Beneath this beastly shape you see
A kind heart beats – the Real Me.
Once I'd a girl to keep me warm
And I threw off this hairy form.
She gave me a kiss and a loving hug
And kept me for a bedroom rug.

Thalarctos maritimus figures in Norse versions of the myth of Beauty and the Beast. The Bestiarist notes: "This is that Monster of ye Boreal Region, North West toward Septentrion, who, though he swim in icy Waters, burneth with Rage. And by Lyeing on his Pelte, Maidens become right amorifick, and in this wanton Guise are pictured gallantly, for his Venerye is in his Haire." Because of this fancied property, it has become necessary to protect the polar bear.

From chilly deeps I rise for air.
A warm reception waits me there,
A rendezvous that rends me quite.
I give him warmth and food and light.

Far from the North my name impresses
Who gave man meat and fire and dresses.

This gentle creature is the prey of Eskimos, who make winter-proof garments of his skin. To quote the Bestiarist: "His flesh they eat, and of his Fatt render Oyle to burn. And his name is a word that signifieth also a Device to impresse in Waxe." Another kind of seal is hunted in more southerly latitudes, but not by Eskimos, and so cruelly that in some countries sealskin is boycotted, to the great injury of trade and the Eskimo's livelihood.

Me you'll quickly determine,
My name rhymes with vermin,
A bloodthirsty, vicious detestable crook.
I'm a slippery sneak
Seven days of the week
And believe me, I've pulled every trick in the book.
And if that's not sufficient to damn me to hell,
Twice a year I'm a cowardly turncoat as well.

Strange metamorphosis! Sublime translation!
With snowy death begins my transformation.
The wheel of Fate revolves. Behold the crook
Adorn the judge, the dowager, the duke.

By mediaeval sumptuary laws, the use of ermine (taken always in winter, when the fur turns white) was restricted to the upper ranks of nobility. The savagery of this little animal is well known, resembling in small (as the Bestiarist puts it) "that Serpent by whom fell our first Mother in Paradise garden."

Believe me, I take not the least credit for
the fact that all women quite madly adore
poor me! I just happen to have these good looks
and get mentioned in all the best-selling books.
It's true most of what they write is pretty cheap —
they run down my morals and call me a creep.
Which, of course, is enough to drive the girls mad!
They love nothing more than an out-and-out cad.

Well, I'm immoral all right. If you want me
I'm yours—if you write out a cheque—easily.
But of course I'm expensive! What d'you think I
am? Breeding and looks, darling, always come high!

The Bestiarist is silent about this animal, which seems not to have been highly esteemed till the nineteenth century. Its willingness to breed in captivity has earned for it a name for promiscuity and for its ranchers fat profits. Only the Russian sable is more costly. By crossing the two species is obtained the *mable* or *sink*, most precious of all furs.

Who's masked and climbs trees?
Who has fingers like these?
Who hollers: Hygiene!
These vittals ain't clean?

Whaddaya say, stranger –
  The Lone Ranger?

The last line seems to allude to a masked horseman, the hero of a television western popular in the 1950's. This is a beast highly compatible with man, surviving even in big cities. Having hands like a citizen, he washes his food carefully before eating it. Of his fur, hats were formerly made for pioneers and, in later days, coats for poor scholars.

The woolverhen or quaquihatch
Has jaws that crush and paws that snatch.
His gluttonous and ugly chaps
Make wreckage of the hunter's traps.
He is a nasty specimen,
The quickahatch or wolveren.

The woolverhatch or quaquihen,
He sadly lacks respect for men.
Trapline and beaver-lodge he seeks,
And havoc's mostly what he wreaks.
He comes to scoff and stays to prey,
The carcajou or quickwahay.

"Quaquihatch or woolverhen" makes an early appearance in the Company's books; also "quiquehatches or wolvereens." Other variants include Quick Hatch, quickhatch, queequeehatch, quickahatch, quickwahay, carcajou. The glutton, *gulo luscus*, wolverine or beaver-eater is the most powerful of the bloodthirsty weasel tribe. The fur is used for trimming the hoods of parkas, since moisture does not condense in it to form frost crystals.

A nation is, because I am.
For Canada I give a dam
And think that I shall never see
A dinner lovely as a tree.

Busy with iv'ry chisels felling
Poplar and birch for food and dwelling,
I build; then under ice I dodge
And busy, labour in my lodge.

My coat for man a cov'ring makes
But that's not all the hunter takes:
His cruel knife cuts off my frolics –
And what is Castor *without* Pollux?

Gentle am I, to man a friend:
His gourmet dish my latter end.

For full information about this animal, long the principal resource of Canada, see the Dissertation on the Beaver that follows.

A DISSERTATION ON THE BEAVER

"A traditional knowledge of the beaver," says a Victorian authority, "is the birthright of every Canadian."

And not only of every Canadian, since the castor or beaver exists in two species, of which one is European and has been known since antiquity.

Consider, then, this exemplary rodent.

The name castor (with Pollux one of the Heavenly Twins of classical myth) springs, perhaps, from the same root as the Latin *castra*, a camp or fortified place, from the creature's marvellous skill in defensive engineering; though some authors derive it from the Greek word for stomach, since its earliest uses, as Hippocrates testifies, were medicinal. The name beaver has a clearer etymology. *Fiber* or *fibir* seems to have been his Latin name; in German *Biber*. The connection with drinking (*cf*. Spanish *beber*, and the English word *beverage*) is obvious.

From earliest times the beaver was renowned for sagacity. His wise foresight in building dams and canals to provide his lodges with underwater approaches could only excite awe and admiration. But these achievements, amazing as they are, are not among those cited by Pliny the Elder as illustrating his cleverness.

What Pliny does report is more remarkable still: that the beaver, hunted for castoreum, a precious medicine contained in his testes, would tear them off (*cf*. English *castrate*) and leave them for his pursuers, escaping with what was yet more precious – his life. Thus the beaver became the Emblem of Prudent Sacrifice.

Castoreum was a nostrum for mental sickness. "Castoreum for the brain," as Sir Francis Bacon puts it. The author of *Castoris animalis naturam et usum medico-chemicum* (1685) recommends castoreum for earache, deafness, gout, and headaches, noting that it "does much good to mad people. It destroys fleas, stops headaches and induces sleep." Other parts of the beaver were of great utility in colic, madness, spasms, epilepsy, apoplexy, and lethargy.

Castoreum had other uses. In time it was found to be an irresistible bait for beaver traps. In 1673 a paper was published in London on "The art of driving away and sinking Whales by Castoreum."

But broadly speaking this essence of the prudent beaver was thought to confer a like prudence on its consumer. The principle is a familiar one in sympathetic magic. Nor can we ignore the significance of beaver-fur's coming into use as a material for hats – in effect, the external application of beaver to the brain.

The point – hitherto overlooked by scholars – is supported by a Jewish tradition that the use of a beaver hat was the secret of Solomon's wisdom. His prescription: "To acquire a prodigious memory and never to forget what he had once read, it was only necessary to wear a hat of the beaver's skin, to rub the head and spine every month with that animal's oil, and to take, once a year, the weight of a gold crown-piece of castoreum."

That the beaver's soft underfur or down is barbed in a way that makes it peculiarly well adapted for manufacturing felt is not, of course, to be overlooked. Yet felt is also used for making boots, and there is no record of beaver-felts being applied successfully in that way. On balance, it becomes clear that the beaver hat is magical in origin.

Pliny's story found its way into the medieval bestiaries. Monkish scholiasts must have been struck with its parable of celibacy. At all events it became common knowledge. Early Committee members of the Hudson's Bay Company could well, with their classical schooling, have read it in the original. It left them with a misapprehension as to the true source of castoreum. They were forever urging their servants to trade "Beaver codds" or "gendering stones."

By the eighteenth century much information had been collected about the beaver. He had become widely known as a tireless woodcutter, the Emblem of Diligence.

Buffon, the great French naturalist, looked at him carefully from the front and observed: "If we consider the anterior parts, no animal is more perfectly adapted for terrestrial life." Then, turning him round to inspect the other end, he added: "And none so well equipped for an acquatic existence, if we look only at the posterior portions."

From this viewpoint, it was also found that the wide, flat tail was a

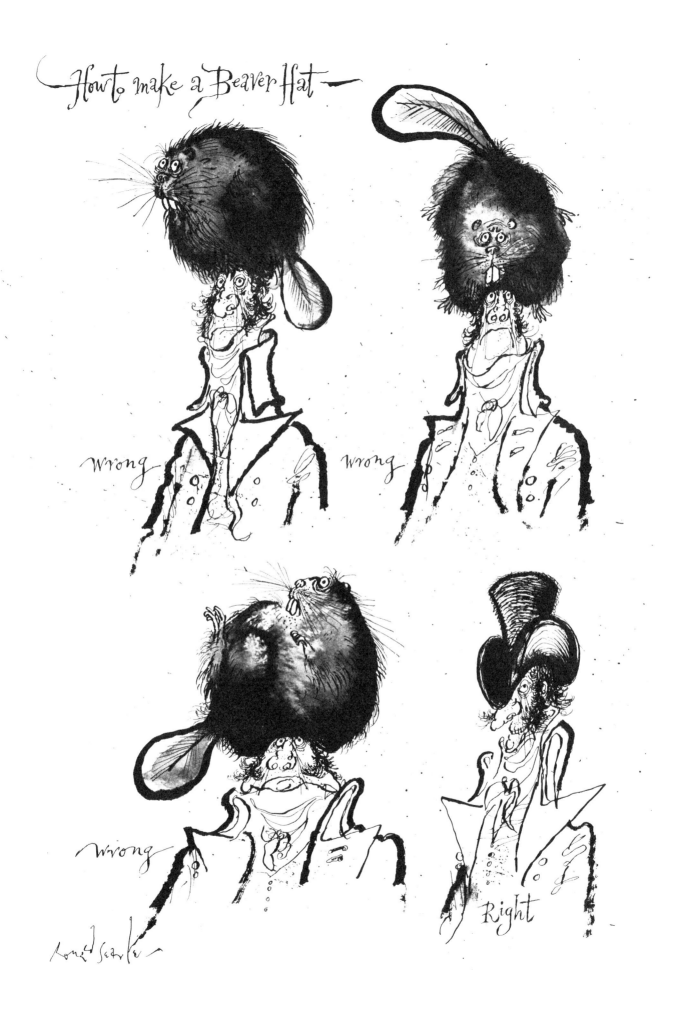

How to make a Beaver Hat —

Wrong

Wrong

Wrong

Right

delicacy. In 1860, no less a visitor than the Earl of Southesk pronounced it palatable. He was only reluctant to name it, referring fastidiously to "the last joints of a beaver's backbone."

By the 1750's, when Malachy Postlethwayt was adapting his *Universal Dictionary of Trade and Commerce* from its French original, beaver science was far advanced. Beavers, he reported, fed only on fish. "In the spring, all those of the same district, or quarter, gather together, and, walking two and two, they go in a body to hunt for animals of their own species; and all those they can catch they lead into their dens, where they make them work like slaves." These, however, were Russian beavers.

Russian, too, were the felt-makers who knew a way to comb the undercoat of wool or down from a beaver-pelt without removing the long guard hairs. It was only necessary to remove the beaver.

Lacking this secret till the eighteenth century, English and French hatters at first preferred to buy their beaver in coat. Worn by Indians till it was ripe, *castor gras* or coat-beaver had already shed its guard-hairs. The glossy underwool was ready for removal and use as felt. Trunk-covers and slippers were made from the skin.

"The process of hat-making," observes wise Postlethwayt, "may appear insipid to those who do not enter into the public utility of bringing every manufactured art to its last perfection." The hatter first makes a cone of felt, then bashes it into shape.

Felt is simply matted hair. Beaver fur, because its hairs are barbed and hook together, mats more tightly than other kinds.

Beaver hats stayed in fashion for long periods. More or less expensive, they were always durable. Fine beavers with furry nap were flaunted by the French. Worn smooth, they were stiffened with gum and sold to the Spanish. The *caballeros* in time passed them on to the Portuguese, who re-made them in smaller sizes for sale in Brazil. Thence the thrifty Portuguese recovered them, full of holes, for sale in Africa.

British postmen were first uniformed in 1793, their issue hat a tall beaver. It lasted them till 1859.

The beaver hat persisted into the late nineteenth century as a headgear for cricketers, who used it to perform the Hat Trick. (Putting a beaver into the hat, instead of taking a rabbit out of it.)

But for elegant wear, the beaver was on its way out. John Hetherington had made his first top hat of plush or silk shag in 1798. By 1851, the year of London's Great Exhibition, English production of silk hats was booming at the rate of 250,000 a year.

The Committee was already planning a revolutionary new use for beaver. In 1843, Secretary Archibald Barclay had written a note about it: "We have been trying some experiments on Beaver, with the view of testing the fitness of the article to be used as a *fur....*"

6.

In which the Honourable Company explores its Territories, seeking Trade and The Northwest Passage.

PRO PELLE CUTEM

The two boys stood where the ship had landed them. It was June 27, 1689, but there was still a barrier of ice along the shore.

The white boy, a Company apprentice, looked north over the dreary expanse of the Barrens, a desert of tundra. Behind him were Churchill and the river.

Their Honours were anxious to develop trade to the northward. And they wanted to know more about their real estate. The Charter was so vague. . . . If the Northwest Passage could be found too, so much the better. But the northern Indians had a reputation for cruelty and treachery. To explore that region was hazardous. It was a man's job.

So they sent a boy to do it.

Henry Kelsey was nineteen. He did not fear the northern Indians. The lad with him was one of them. Besides, Kelsey spoke their language. He meant to find and invite them to Churchill to trade.

The Indian boy was peering anxiously along the shore. He wanted to move inland at once.

Kelsey knew what he was worrying about. He was afraid of Huskies or Usquemews. These Esquimaughs, however you spelled them, were mortal enemies of the Indians.

Kelsey's shipmates, who knew them, had complained only about their smell. That was a laugh too. Everyone in these parts, including the white men, was nasty in his person. Why pick on Askimays?

Lugging their samples, the boys trudged inland. They were horribly plagued by mosquitoes.

Kelsey made notes. One day he would be a writer, maybe even a poet. "July 2. At noon it rained hard having no shelter but ye heavens for a Cannope nor no wood to make a fire."

He was no hell at punctuation. But he could spell as well as any Company man: "July 9. Spyed two Buffillo and we Killed one." The observant boy added that their horns "joyn together upon their forehead & so come down ye side of their head and turn up."

What he was describing was an Asian water-buffalo, seldom seen so far north. Had he, in fact, reached the Indies? Evidently not. Taxonomists insist that the animals were musk oxen and Kelsey their discoverer.

The boys underwent fearful hardships on their six-week trip. But though they covered more than two hundred miles before they got back to Churchill, they saw no customers.

They found the Governor distracted. Some clot had gone and burnt down the fort.

After listening to Kelsey's report, he ventured an obscure joke.

"You had your labour for your travel!"

The boy laughed dutifully.

Travel, travail – the sort of gag that might come in handy to a travelling salesman. Or a poet.

A year later, the boy got his chance to show what he could do with words.

He was sent out on a sales trip from York Factory. He was to travel westward in search of the Stonybroke Indians or Assinine Poets. With him, as guide and mentor, was the Captain of the Poets.

Riding on a smile and a canoe-shine, he moved at the reckless speed of six hundred miles a month. He went "chearfully" because of an advance of salary. Arriving at the Pas, or Lake Winnipeg, or Cedar Lake (he was not sure which), he solved the problem by naming it Dering's Point. Dering was the Deputy Governor he hoped would approve his advance.

He set out his samples and puffed the *calamity* with all comers. He did his best to promote peace between his own trading Indians and the Poets.

His efforts were not very successful.

Yet his journey was by no means in vain. He gave the poets the old sales pitch. What was more, he learned to write Assinine poetry himself:

> *Then up ye River I with heavy heart*
> *Did take my way & from all English part*
> *To live among ye Natives of this place*
> *If god permits me for one two years space.*

Kelsey was the first English salesman to call on prairie accounts.

He found the plains teeming with bison, the herds stalked by grizzly bears. Reckless as ever of taxonomy, he wrote:

> *The one is a black a Buffillo great*
> *Another is an outgrown Bear wch is good meat.*

"He is a man's food," Kelsey went on. Then, remembering his own close call with two grizzlies, added, "And he makes food of man."

He had managed to avoid being made food by shooting both bears.

In 1692 Kelsey returned to York Factory with a good fleet of Indians and furs. He was now a veteran traveller, a hardened poet.

His Journals were sent to London – where they got into unauthorised hands.

But they had made his name. Twenty years later, the Committee wrote commending his devotion to letters: "You doe well to Educate the men in Literature. . . ."

After the Peace of Utrecht, Their Honours thought once more of expansion to the Northward. Exploring that region would be hazardous as ever. James Knight left them in no doubt about that.

"Them natives to the Norward," he wrote them, "are more Savage and brute-like than these and will drink blood and eat raw flesh and fish and loves it as well as some does Strong Drink."

Once again, it was a man's job. A task for an experienced traveller and seaman in the full vigour of his prime. Henry Kelsey, Knight's Deputy, was the obvious choice.

This time they did not send a boy. They sent Knight, now in his seventies and complaining bitterly about his health – colds, weak knees, gout, ague.

Knight forced them to send him.

The old carpenter came over to London and browbeat the gentlemen in person. Kelsey? The fellow was untrustworthy. Besides, the idea of an expedition in search of gold, copper, and the Northwest Passage was Knight's own idea. No one was going to take it away from him.

He knew these London merchants. He had been Lake's right-hand man, lobbying at Utrecht. He was better than any of them. When they had tried to get him to submit weekly messing accounts from York he had scornfully refused: "I believe it was a thing hardly ever done – a man above 1,000 leagues off to tell what he eats a-days!"

Toiling to rebuild Churchill in the brief, sweltering summer of 1717, the old seadog had slapped at mosquitoes, fumed at the Committee.

He had often heard those sleek businessmen say they had a good mind to come over here. He'd love to see them spend their summer vacation right on this spot where the fort was going up! It would teach them to set a little more value on men's lives. The place was littered with human bones.

Jens Munk, the Dane, had wintered here a century earlier. Only three of his sixty-four men had survived. Here the forests petered out in a sprinkling of stunted jackpines, branchless to the icy north, giving way to wastes of tundra. Winter smothered it in darkness almost around the clock. Summer brought swarms of flies with the midnight sun. A cold, comfortless place. Only the white whales made it profitable. They sported about the sloop, nuzzled the canoes.

"I never see such a miserable place in my life!" Knight raged.

He made the Committee feel it was all their fault.

No one dared ask why, if he hated the north so much, he was proposing to go still farther north into the unknown.

They gave him his ships.

Early in June, 1719, the *Albany* and *Discovery* slipped moorings and set sail from London.

In command of the expedition was James Knight.

His old bones ached with rheumatism. But his heart burned like a boy's with gold fever. He was sailing north to discover the fabled Straits of Anyan, to unlock at long last the secret of the Northwest Passage.

Knight was never heard of again. He and his Captains with their ships and crews vanished into the vast silence of the Arctic.

Years afterwards, Company sailors found wreckage of two ships in a cove at the Southeast end of Marble Island. Eskimos remembered how the white men had succeeded in getting ashore; how they had built shelters of clay and moss; how, at last, one by one, they had starved to death.

The second summer after the wreck, two famished survivors had been seen standing on a rock, looking earnestly to seaward. After a long time, they had sat down together and wept bitterly.

Kelsey was in those waters that summer, in the *Prosperous*. It could have been her sails the dying men were watching.

No wonder they were crying.

"Wanst the master takes a hoult on a notion," said the butler at Castle Dobbs, "he don't let go. Do ye mind the time he was on about the Rory Bory Alehouse?"

The cook scowled. "The what?"

"The Northern Lights, woman!"

"Will I ever forget it!"

"Faith, now 'tis the Northwest Passage! Your man is off of his head entirely. 'Tis Northwest Passage morning noon and night. If he riz up from his bed in the dark of night, 'tis Northwest Passage he'd be giving out!"

"And amn't I after sweeping it meself!"

Arthur Dobbs was Mayor of Carrickfergus, Surveyor General of Ireland and a friend of Sir Robert Walpole. Naturally Sir Bibye Lake listened to him.

He turned pale when his visitor mentioned his obsession. Dobbs would have it that the Charter required the Company to look for the Northwest Passage.

Sir Bibye thought of his old friend James Knight.

"We did make an attempt," he said faintly, "about eleven years ago. It cost us six thousand pound, two ships, and some of our best men. . . ."

Dobbs brushed this aside. He talked on, fierce and persuasive. It was frightening how much he knew about Company affairs.

Sir Bibye did his best to put him off. There was talk of war these days – even Walpole could not ignore it. The Company had to concentrate on defence. Once the great stone fort at Churchill was built, he would be glad to come in on any scheme. . . .

Dobbs went home and brooded over this, moodily rack-renting his peasants while he thought up a new approach.

War did break out in 1739 – over the ownership of Jenkins' ear. The campaigns against the Spanish were so badly bungled Walpole had to resign. Stone-masons laboured ineptly at Fort Prince of Wales, Churchill, but the work, begun in 1731, would not be finished till 1771.

Dobbs couldn't wait that long.

He began a twenty-year attack on the Hudson's Bay Company.

If they would not look for the Northwest Passage, he would. Luring Captain Middleton out of their employ, he persuaded the Admiralty to send him with two ships to the Arctic. Middleton looked all over for the Passage without success. Home again, he announced flatly that it did not exist.

Dobbs was enraged. Middleton was hiding something from him – the Northwest Passage. Obviously the man was in the pay of the Company.

He began a pamphlet war with the unlucky captain. Remarks, criticisms, poison-pen letters, answers, replies to answers, answers to replies,

The Polemics of Arthur Dobbs Esquire

rebuttals of ripostes to answers in reply to answers whizzed back and forth.

Dobbs even wrote a book on the countries adjoining Hudson Bay. He got much of his information from a latter-day Radisson called LaFrance. ("A refugee, a runagade, an illiterate, a French Indian," sneered the Company's Captain Coats, forgetting the origins of his own livelihood.)

Dobbs made the outrageous claim that the prairies were fit for settlement. Only the Company blocked the way to empire. Parliament should repeal its Charter.

The Irishman formed his own company to find the Passage. Failure of its two-ship voyage of discovery in 1746 daunted him not at all. In 1749 he succeeded in getting Parliament to investigate the Hudson's Bay Company.

The Adventurers were on trial. They were accused of not exploring their territory, of sleeping by the seaside, of maltreating Indians and their own servants.

It was true Indians and Company men were sometimes flogged or clapped in irons. Parliament could see nothing wrong in that. Worse things happened every day in His Majesty's ships. In England the gallows, the rack, the thumbscrew were in daily use.

The charge of failing to explore proved harder to answer. Kelsey's journal would have helped, but the original could not be found. Dobbs's counsel managed to cast doubt on the genuineness of the summary filed in its stead.

In 1926 the original turned up at Castle Dobbs, Carrickfergus.

The Company survived, its Charter intact.

Dobbs renewed his assault with a proposal to buy it out with Irish revenues. The Company's territories could be taken over as an Irish possession garrisoned with Irish regiments.

This was too much. George II sent for Dobbs.

"Go out and govern North Carolina," the King said.

What Samuel Hearne hated about Churchill's Governor Moses Norton was his common propensity to the unfair sex. He was a debauchee who wanted every woman in the country for himself. Leaving none for Sam.

Hearne was bored. Bored with Norton, bored with Churchill and its idiotic fort, bored with meticulously carving his name on a rock by the wharf.

He was glad to get out and look for the Northwest Passage on foot. Disaster-prone, he did not get far – not till he met Matonabbee.

"What you need," the Indian told him, "is women."

This Matonabbee certainly was the most sociable, kind, and sensible Indian Hearne had ever met.

He had seven wives, big as grenadiers, every one of them laden down with goods and gear.

"Women," Matonabbee explained, "were made for labour. One of them can carry or haul as much as two men. They also pitch our tents, make and mend our clothing, keep us warm at nights."

Hearne took it all to heart.

"Women," Matonabbee went on, "though they do everything, are maintained at a trifling expense. For as they always stand cook, the very licking of their fingers in scarce times is sufficient for their subsistence."

At his third sortie from the fort, in December 1770, Governor Norton gave Hearne no seven-gun salute.

Instead, the seven wives of Matonabbee led off at a brisk five miles a day. It was dark, mostly, and by the time the days had begun to lengthen, Hearne had got used to the ladies.

Hearne sets out ...

An obedient sailor all his life, he was content to let Matonabbee take charge.

They were to find the Coppermine River and follow it in search of ore and the famous Northwest Passage.

They walked westward over bleak rocks and hills, gathering dry moss to make fires, feasting when they had luck shooting caribou or muskox, at other times starving or taking fish from the innumerable lakes.

All winter long they drifted West.

In April they turned North, the women grunting under loads of wood and birchbark collected in the forests. These would be used to make canoes.

Presently the women were left behind. The kind Indian and about two hundred of his countrymen had decided to attack their enemies the Eskimos.

Hearne's protests were so badly received he quickly changed his tune. He was in the hands of these people.

The sun shone day and night.

Strange Indians with copper ornaments were overjoyed to see Hearne, their first white man. How ugly he was! His hair like a buffalo's tail, his eyes like a gull's, his skin pale as water-logged meat!

Within a generation, contact with this visitor's unlovely race was to shatter the Indians with smallpox.

In July, Hearne came, after all his wandering and privations, to the long-wished-for goal of his quest – the Coppermine River.

He saw at a glance it was useless for navigation: all shoals and rapids. His heart sank.

Worse was to come. The kind and sensible Matonabbee and his friends had found an Eskimo camp.

Hearne looked on, anguished but powerless, while his comrades fell on the sleeping Eskimos and butchered them.

Their Honours would not like this one bit.

A whole century of admonitions was nattering in the ears of their faithful servant. *It doth advantage them nothing to kill and destroy one a nother That thereby they may soe weaken themselves that the wild raveneus beasts may grow to numerous for them & Destroy those that Survive.* . . . Company men were to make peace among the natives. Hearne had let down the side.

After this, it was no fun finding the vaunted copper mine – a jumble of rocks and gravel. Four hours of rummaging yielded only one lump of metal.

Arrived at last at the Arctic, the first white man to reach it overland saw only that it was jammed with ice in mid July.

If there was a Northwest Passage, it was useless.

7

In which is offered a
History of Transportation
in their Honours' Territories
with
Hints for Travellers

The Company was still working tirelessly toward the concept of department stores.

But the essential communications media had not been developed. It still took two years to send and receive a letter from head office. Nor had communications theory yet made its appearance, though when it did come, astonishing the global village, it arose from studies of the fur trade and its effects.

In the fullness of time, the Canadian fur empire would beget its greatest historian and theorist, Harold A. Innis. And Innis would beget Marshall McLuhan.

The McLuhan method ignores chronology, disdaining connected argument. It presents a mosaic of bright bits and pieces, like the front page of a newspaper.

MARSHALL THE FACTS

The Company depended on sea communication, protected by naval weaponry.

Except in the mosquito season, sea-ice closed Hudson Bay to navigation. Charts were unreliable, compasses temperamental and dead reckoning often dead wrong. Early ships bound for the Bay were small, slow and fragile. Seldom bigger than sixty tons burthen, they were often wrecked. But they did not need docking facilities and were easily repaired. Bales of high-priced furs made handy cargo. So did bales of the kind of goods demanded by nomadic customers – nothing more bulky than a nine-pound kettle.

THE MEDIUM WAS THE MESSDECK

The content of the ship was unimportant. Messdeck conditions were frightful, crews tended to be riffraff – Scotch, Dutch, and many boyes. *Lacking vitamin C, which had not been invented, they were scurvy jack-tars.*

Ship was a total environment, an extension of the human skin. The oak hull was a collective garment enclosing not just an individual but a whole crew. *Pro pelle cutem* – a skin (human) for a skin (wooden overcoat). Thus each member exchanged private identity for a corporate personality.

The first thing sailors did on landing was to reproduce this total environment on shore. A ship's bell marked the hours. Wind and weather were anxiously observed. Shipboard discipline was enforced.

Ship was the dominant medium.

As snow was to Eskimo, ship was to empire.

Eskimo had scores of words for snow. In sea-farers' English, the word *ship* was reserved for full-rigged three-masters, replete with royals, topsails, skysails, and studdingsails. The Company's many types of ship had as many names. *Ketch* and *dogger* were two-masters. Much favoured by sailors was the three-masted *pink*, rigged square on fore and main only, with a lateen on the mizzen.

There were also frigates, hoys, capers, sloops, shallops – each and every one of them a grand old sight with its grand old canvas flying like shirts on a clothes-line.

FAR-CALLED, OUR NAVIES MELT AWAY/ ON DUNE & HEADLAND SINKS THE FUR
(Rudyard Kipling)

Once wooden walls were replaced by iron, Britannia's sea power began to rust.

The introduction of steam paddle-wheels was the beginning of the end. With the screw steamer, the art of seamanship was ruined.

All this, of course, was the result of the invention of printing, which had led first to the Reformation and the rise of capitalism, then to the Industrial Revolution, railways, telegraphs, and Canadian Confederation.

The invention of the typewriter, on the other hand, led to new forms of weaponry such as the bikini and the miniskirt.

THE SURVIVORS LIVE THROUGH BORROWING CULTURAL TRAITS OF PEOPLES WHO HAVE ALREADY WORKED OUT A CIVILIZATION SUITABLE TO THE NEW ENVIRONMENT
(Harold A. Innis)

The Indians, being tribal and preliterate, depended largely on words for communication. But they also made eloquent use of bows-and-arrows, stone axes, and tobacco smoke.

Certain tribal media were new to the white man.

The snowshoe was an extension of the human foot, enabling its wearer to run over deep snow at a smart trot. Profound disturbances in sensibility resulted from this modification. French wood runners who adopted it became independent of colonial authority. Farther south, English racqueteers were so changed by the new medium they dumped perfectly good tea into Boston Harbour instead of drinking it.

Dog was another medium affecting Indians and Eskimos. Mexican Indians used a hairless breed with high body-temperature as a foot warmer. In all parts of the continent dog was eaten. Prairie tribes tied poles to it with loads on them. Known as a *travois*, this was an attempt to invent the dog-cart that got no farther than the shafts. Other Indian tribes, as well as the Eskimos, used the dog to haul sleds.

Sled dogs were harnessed in teams, using either the line hitch or the fan hitch. Not that it made much difference which hitch. There was always a hitch of some kind, often a bitch.

Dog-sledding was a wretched occupation inducing foul temper and even madness in the driver. Though dogs would eat anything, including the hand that fed them, it was the custom to regale them on working days with 120 frozen fish. Tedious hours were spent in winter catching 120 frozen fish for each dog. In summer their masters let them starve.

Dog communication, adopted by the white man, led to a variant of noble competition known as dog-eat-dog.

THE MUSKET BALL WAS PURE INFORMATION

The fur trade was an interface between two technologies.

Each was changed by the other.

The Indian replaced his stone-age weaponry with the gun, hatchet, knife, and awl of the trader. With these new media the Micmac of Nova Scotia quickly communicated with the Beothuk of Newfoundland, who have not been heard from since.

The white man learned the correct use of dogs and women. He learned to dress warmly and prevent scurvy by drinking spruce beer. He learned to impersonate the female moose, luring the male to destruction. He learned to smoke tobacco and to use Indian food. Above all, he learned to travel inland to the Shield.

INTERVIEWER: ARE YOU SOME KIND OF COMMUNIST
PIERRE ELLIOTT TRUDEAU: NO—I'M A CANOEIST

Inland, canoe was the dominant medium.

Canoe was an extension of the human posterior.

Canadians took to it to prove that you could too make a buck by sitting on your backside.

Light and strong, the Indian canoe was a twenty-foot shell of birch–bark, lacking a keel, but reinforced with cedar ribs and thwarts. Seams were water-proofed with fir-tree gum. One or two men could carry it overland wherever the flow of water was troubled with dangerous rapids or falls (*portages*).

French paddlers quickly adapted it to the needs of the inland fur trade. They made it bigger and stronger without sacrificing lightness. Large

Transportation

freight canoes carried as many as twenty-five men. Twenty of these canoes made up a brigade.

Each carried its *bourgeois* or door-to-door salesman.

The paddlers did the work. Fuelled with lyed corn and pork fat, fifty songs a day was nothing to them. They could carry, paddle, walk, and sing with any man.

Propped on its side on shore, the canoe made a rude overnight shelter.

Not that the paddlers used it much. They were all in the woods looking for Indian girls.

Along the canoe routes appeared a new nation of halfbreeds known as Métis.

IGDLORSSUALIORTUGSSARSIUMAROQ (Eskimo word meaning "He wants to find a man who can build a large house.")

Scarcely less rude than an upturned canoe were the native shelters.

The wigwam, filled with smoke, was downright insulting.

The teepee of the Plains Indians, though its dressed skin exterior was handsomely decorated, was not much better.

Much more sophisticated was the igloo or *igdlo*, the snow house of the Eskimo. Independently of Committeeman Wren, the Eskimo had invented the dome – an abstraction from the female breast.

Arctic temperatures fall as low as sixty degrees below zero. Inside the igdlo the temperature could be raised by as much as ninety degrees – to the freezing point of water.

To raise it higher would have melted the house. Survival inside the igdlo required propinquity and warmth of temperament. Igdlo called for id-glow.

SLICE UPON SLAB OF LUSCIOUS GOOSEBOSOM
(James Joyce, *Finnegans Wake*)

Portable food had to be found for paddlers. Fish gave poor mileage. Lyed corn and lard were better. Best of all was pemmican.

Pemmican was invented by the plains Indians. Meat was first cut into strips and dried, then pounded to dust. Mixed with berries, it was poured into buffalo-hide bags along with melted fat. Paddlers had to have their cholesterol.

From time to time they dropped dead. Whenever this happened, rude crosses were erected at portages.

THE HORSE IS A CAMEL
DESIGNED BY A GRANDEE

The Spanish introduced rude horses to Mexico in the sixteenth century. Two hundred years later, chivalry or horse-culture had found its way north to the prairies.

The horse was an extension of the human legs. The Blackfoot Conspiracy adopted it in an attempt to keep their toes clean. Hitched to a *travois*, a horse could carry more than a dog or even a woman. This increased Blackfoot demand for trade goods.

Chivalry brought new violence to noble competition. Indians were now gentlemen. No longer pedestrian, even cops had to become gentlemen to deal with them. This was cleverly achieved by inserting a horse under each of their rumps and dressing them in red coats and boy-scout hats.

The old ways are best.

The first necessity is to keep warm. Early Company servants sometimes froze to death. Survivors had learned the secret of keeping warm: BE DIRTY.

Nothing is more calorific than a thick coating of filth.

The trader's hands and face were black as a chimney-sweep's, his clothes greasy as a butcher's.

The English merchant class had begun to experiment with washing in warm water during the 1660's. It would be a long time before common people tried anything so dangerous.

Indians occasionally took a sweat bath, followed by a wash in fresh snow. "Such methods," a Company man noted disapprovingly in the mid-eighteenth century, "with Some Europians wou'd be present Death."

Samuel Hearne, however, carried soap with him into the Barrens.

The well-dressed Hudsonian wore three pairs of wool socks under soft moccasins, a pair of cloth stockings over another of worsted, buckskin breeches, flannel shirt, and double-lined waistcoat under a beaver cape. His face was covered with a duffel chin-clout with holes for eyes and nose. Over all was a shapeless beaver topcoat reaching almost to the ground, called a toggy.

Toggied, blackfaced, and piratically bearded, the traders' hairy appearance could lead to misunderstanding. In September, 1800, three grizzly bears tried to climb into a York boat with the Company's Peter Fidler and crew. "These," he primly reported, "was the most daring Bears any of us had ever seen."

Skin clothes are recommended. Wear two layers, the skinside inside on the outside, the inside outside next the skinside inside. Rub well with whale or walrus blubber. For care and upkeep they require Eskimo women.

For travel in sage-brush country, dress as for the Sind Desert. Solar topees should be lined with foil. Camels are not recommended, however, as they dislike mud. They slip, split their breast-bones, and break up. A spare breast-bone may be carried, but this is a desperate measure.

Yaks, too, are unsuitable. They stampede at the smell of Europeans. Excellent on snow, they are strong and reliable, but so slow that there can be no question of double-marching.

Dog whips are best made of white whale skin with lash about eight feet longer than the traces. The boredom of long marches drives Huskies to eat traces and whip if precautions are not taken. To prevent this, break the dog's back teeth from both sides of the lower jaw. Watch for the S.P.C.A.

To turn left, shout *Aouk!*; to turn right, *Huhk Ehk!*; to stop, *Wuu!* It is vital to know your *Aouk* from your *Huhk Ehk*. Practise daily.

To stop a wholesale fight take a running jump into the mass of dogs, who immediately disperse. (If not, sue the Royal Geographical Society, which recommends the procedure.)

To make bannocks.

Take mouldy wheat flour and knead into a thick dough with water or melted snow. When grayish from handling, roll into a ball, then crush into a dry frying-pan. Scorch over a wood fire. Once it is burnt on both sides (the authentic bannockburn), sprinkle with woodash and serve.

To make delicious pemmican.

Take one buffalo and proceed as for caribou pemmican.

If in an area where buffalo or caribou is not easily obtainable, a small quantity of simple pemmican may be prepared in the privacy of the home as follows:

Find some old, dried-out ends of meat and cut off the hard outside crusts. Pound these to dust in a mortar. Add mouldy raisins, buckshot, and a jug of melted, rancid animal fat. Sprinkle with long black hairs and poodle-clippings. Stir. Pour into an old shoe and refrigerate. After six months a greenish fur will have grown on the pemmican. Remove and keep this: it is pemmicillin.

Pemmican is rich in nutriment, containing 180 calories per ounce. Do not remove them.

8.

In which the Honourable Company awakes to a new Challenge. As the Nor'Westers cross the Continent

The Company had been accused of falling asleep by the frozen sea.

They were not asleep. They had heard every word the rude fellows were saying. And, through it all, had gone on making profits.

Summer after summer, fleets of Indian jobbers paddled their furs down river to shop at the Bay.

The department-store concept was germinating.

As well as the Trading-room there were departments. In the Slops shop the men could buy sloppy clothing on credit. The Provisions store held beer, brandy, confectionery, cheese, chocolate, etc. Other departments included Armourers', Bricklayers', Carpenters', Coopers', Gunners', Harpooners', Sawyers', Shipwrights', Smiths'.

The Factory store stocked, among other oddments, baskets, books, and bottles; candles, chairs, and one flag, Union, large.

Making lists of everything was the clerks' simplest chore. They had also to keep – as always – Exact Journals, practise Utmost Frugality, and make fair copies of obsequious letters to London.

There were ships to be turned round, firewood to be cut, migrating geese and partridge to be massacred, plucked, and put up in salt, buildings to construct and mend. All this had to be done in summer – which was also the shopping season.

The Governors were tormented by flies and helpful letters from the Committee.

Sometimes Their Honours wanted to raise the Standard of Trade, though they knew "it must be done discreetly without disgusting the Natives."

It was important not to give a Disgust.

In the Age of Reason, Their Honours went all progressive. They tried to introduce medicare in 1738 by offering free treatment for venereal disease. Bayside authorities protested on behalf of the surgeons: "a hardship on the profession." Besides, as Governor James Isham at York put it: "We humbly conceive this will be in some measure opening the door for licentiousness."

Their Honours relented. Their servants were licentious enough.

Attempts to keep them chaste had failed.

Hudson Bay was a disconsolate place – and Indian girls were frisky and bewitching when young. Much of what the Company knew about its country had been learned from them, the sleeping dictionaries of empire. One striking young woman had been Knight's best informant. This Thanadelthur had taken charge of an exploration party nominally under William Stuart's command, making peace between warring Crees and her own Chipewyan.

Cree girls were hot stuff. "No accomplishments whatever in a man," Hearne reported, "is sufficient to conciliate the affections, or preserve the

chastity of a Southern Indian woman." Isham praised their half breed
offspring: "as fine Children as one wou'd Desire to behold." And "pretty
Numerious."

The English lived under discipline; even their private letters were
censored. They envied the free life of the Indians. This was, as one of them
wistfully expressed it, "most certainly that freedom of nature and in-
dependancy which the ancient poets dreamed of."

In the winter-long nights under the pale banners of the aurora,
thinking about all this drove many a man to drink.

Food was heavy and monotonous. Fish for breakfast, salt goose for dinner. Always. In summer the goose was eaten fresh with dandelion salad. As Imperial trade-links improved, curry-powder would be imported from India to hot it up. All this goose was washed down with compulsory spruce beer.

Recruiting men for this life at Company pay-rates was a perennial headache for the Committee.

They scoured the remoter parts of the British Isles for suitably desperate candidates. Charity boys from London's bluecoat and graycoat schools served well enough. But the Committee settled at last on Orkneymen.

Anything was better than living in the Orkneys. Orkneymen were ideal. They were described as close, prudent, quiet people, strictly faithful to their employers.

Best of all, they were sordidly avaricious.

Competition from pedlars was forcing the Company to send salesmen inland, set up shops in the interior. Between the conquest of Quebec and 1774, when Cumberland House was established on the Saskatchewan, there was an average of three up-country trips a year.

The Company's Anthony Henday came in sight of the Rockies in 1755. His report of having seen Blackfoot horsemen on the plains was ridiculed. His much later claim that up-country Indians were warmly attached to the French Canadians impressed no one.

Pedlars! *A parcel of lazey fellows, fit to eat the divel and smook his mother.* Even their booty was of no account. Their Honours referred loftily to "their indifferent and stagey Furrs."

The French show-offs had one final shock in store for the Company.

In 1782 a squadron of French ships, allies of the revolting Americans to the South, appeared off Fort Prince of Wales, and pretended they were fit to capture it.

Samuel Hearne was Governor. He had not even known there was a war on.

It was true the fort was impregnable. Forty years a-building, it was the last word in defensive engineering. Ramparts of costly masonry bristled with forty-five big guns. Hearne could muster barely enough defenders to man two of them.

Veteran of more than one sea battle, he knew hopeless odds when he saw them. He surrendered at once.

The French commander was much relieved. His men were dying like flies from typhus and scurvy.

Somehow they found strength to wreck the beautiful fort.

Next year Hearne was back at Churchill building a new one, this time of green timber.

The British has lost their revolting Americans. But they insisted on keeping Canada and the Bay.

"Englishman!" the chief was saying, "it is to you that I speak, and I demand your attention!"

The chief was a terrifying sight in his warpaint. More impressive, he was promoting a new Pontiac.

It was 1763 and Pontiac was leading the tribes on the warpath.

The pedlar was listening all right.

"Englishmen, although you have conquered the French, you have not conquered us! We are not your slaves. These lakes, these woods and mountains were left to us by our ancestors. They are our inheritance; and we will part with them to none!"

After this, the pedlar was relieved to learn that all they wanted was his trade goods and a taste of English milk – the rum he carried for premiums.

This pedlar, Alexander Henry, was a Yankee, one of the first of a new breed challenging the Company.

He made it to Fort Michilimacinacinac (pronounced Mishmash) just in time for the massacre.

He was surprised to see Indians playing lacrosse in front of the fort.

The English garrison, always suckers for field-sports, looked on, languidly applauding.

"Oh, good shot, sir!"

"Jolly well let alone, sir!"

There was a breathless hush in the close, a bumping pitch, and a blinding light.

The ball arced lazily in the summer air. It rolled near to the palisade, both maddened and tumultuous teams in full cry after it.

Near the open gate, they snatched tomakawks from under their squaws – and charged whooping into the fort.

Obviously rotten sports.

Henry did not enjoy seeing them chopping up Englishmen. Nor was it nice to observe at such close quarters the technique of scalping.

He was into a new kind of ballgame altogether. Still, in private enterprise you expected to get your hair mussed once in a while.

Right now he had to find someone to hide him.

A French pawnbroker refused to make a deal with Henry. Luckily his slave-girl – a Pawnee, in fact – took pity.

This escape and many another Henry owed to good public relations. Customers were always glad to do him a favour.

He found his way to Montreal. There he found associates who shared his sales philosophy, his hard-earned understanding of the customer.

The plural of Mac in Gaelic is *Mic* – and in Montreal the *Mic* had inherited the earth.

McTavish, McGillivray, Mackenzie, McDonald, McGill, MacIntosh,

McLeod, Grant, Fraser – the clans had taken over the St. Lawrence fur empire.

Trouserless Highlanders with beards like sporrans, gaunt ex-Frasers with hungry others newly landed from the ruined crofts and moors. In a single generation their pride and effrontery had made them lords of the lakes and forests.

Dukes of the dinner tables, they were pillars of Montreal society as in time they would be columns in its telephone directory.

Their eyes were cold as the glint of Culloden steel, their blood fiery with unblended usquebaugh, elbows and knees knobby as the oatmeal porridge that fed them. Shedding auld-country pretences – Young Pretender, Old Pretender, and the rest of it – they set to and exploited the conquest. They were joined by a remnant of French on the make and, after the revolting Americans cut loose in 1776, a handful of Yanks on the run.

These were the men who took over the pedlars and paddlers. Riding on the backs of their singing *voyageurs*, now Imperial coolies, they fought and clawed their way into the fur country of the Northwest.

To get so far required capital. They had to pool resources, combining in large, loose partnerships.

None was larger or looser than the North West Company.

This ferocious syndicate would emerge as the arch-rival of the Adventurers of England for the riches of the receding frontier.

Its first princes were Simon the Marquis McTavish, famed for his love of girls and oysters, Jimmy the College McGill, and Athabasca Pete, alias Peter Pond, a Yankee badman who lived to beat three murder raps. Alexander Henry was proud to be accepted as an equal by men like these.

He knew what kind of ball game he was into this time.

By the 1870's the Syndicate had carried trade and smallpox to the Athabasca country from forward bases at the head of the Great Lakes.

Athabasca Pete, a compulsive salesman, had arrived in 1778 and traded the clothes off his back. Only prudery stopped him from selling the clothes off his front as well. He had managed to break through the cordon of Indian jobbers and middlemen to the innocents who actually produced the furs.

That year a couple of the boys poisoned a customer by spiking his grog with laudanum in the Eagle Hills. The Indians waited till spring to kill them.

The men from the Bay, too, had at last invaded the Shield country in earnest. They tended the Indian plague-victims, *cut to the heart* at their suffering.

Bay agents were shadowing every move of the Syndicate. Instructed to give no insult nor take any, at Cumberland House the Scotch factor had grimly warned off an Irish Nor'Wester.

"Scotchmen can kill as well as Irishmen can."

But the lordly Nor'Westers were too quick and aggressive for their rivals. They were, after all, their own bosses. The Bay men, however tough and diligent, were servants.

Athabasca Pete comfortably set up shop in his new district. In 1787 he was joined by Wee Sandy Mackenzie.

Wee Sandy was a braw, bonny lad of twenty-three, with the soulful eyes of a spaniel.

He dreamed of the Pacific.

In June, 1789, he slipped away from Lake Athabasca to find it.

For paddler-power he had four singing *voyageurs*, a German, three Indians, and an assortment of four wives.

They came to Great Slave Lake and followed an unknown river, none knew whither.

Strange Indians fled in terror at their approach or stopped to warn of horrid monsters in the way.

The great river carried them to the land of midnight sun.

Mackenzie looked out into the fogs of the estuary. Whales sported among the sea ice.

The Hyperborean Ocean! Not the Pacific.

Sick with frustration, he named the unlucky stream the River of Disappointment.

It was, of course, the Mackenzie.

It was an odd error to make. Determined not to repeat it, he went to England to buy better surveying instruments.

Armed with these and a course in mapping, he made a fresh start from Athabasca in May, 1793. This time he followed the Peace River all the way to the Rockies.

His 25-foot canoe carried ten souls and three thousand pounds of baggage. It was badly damaged on the way and, after portaging it over the Great Divide, he had his men build a new one. This he cached at the headwaters of the Fraser for the return trip.

Taking an old Indian trail to Friendly Village on the Bella Coola, his seven paddlers scrambled over the mountains with ninety-pound packs. The two Indians panted under half that weight.

Wordsworth had not yet published his *Lyrical Ballads* and Wee Sandy was not conditioned to admire mountain scenery. He saw wild and unwholesome forests, frightful precipices, gloomy caverns, rugged and ridgy escarpments.

The heat was dreadful. And then the rain.

The Friendly Villagers lent dugouts for the last run down the Bella Coola to the ocean.

Hostile tribesmen shouted, "Macoubah! Macoubah!"

Mackenzie did not understand. Did they mean Vancouver? But it had not yet been founded; besides, it was farther South.

Borrowing a lipstick, he left his mark on a rock.

"Alexander Mackenzie, from Canada, by land, the twenty-second of July, one thousand seven hundred and ninety-three."

Mackenzie nearing the pacific coast

David Thompson was the most promising apprentice the Company had had in years. He wrote a clear, neat hand, the first accurate speller ever to reach the shores of Hudson Bay.

It was August, 1790.

His face shone with effort, his squat form crouched over the letter he was writing. A Welsh recruit from London's graycoat school, the former Dai ap Thomas was a memorable sight as his deepset eyes shifted in search of inspiration.

Only this morning he had cut his long black hair with the help of a suet-bowl. The bangs all but covered his short nose.

He was addressing Their Honours in the customary report as the end of his seven-year apprenticeship approached.

"I have served you with the utmost Fidelity," he pointed out. A broken leg had confined him to desk duties. He had been learning the Theory and Practice of Practical Astronomy. He was entitled to a complete set of clothes. In their place he requested a brass sextant by Dolland, a pair of parallel glasses, and some nautical almanacs.

Their Honours made him a present of everything he asked for, along with an encouraging letter.

Philip Turnor, the Company's best surveyor, taught him everything he knew.

An exemplary pupil, Thompson never once smoked or swore. When it came time to take a woman to bear his dusky race, he married her in church. All sixteen little ones would be legitimate. In everything he did, he was always right.

He was right to quit the Company when his boss called a halt to surveying. He was right to join the Nor'Westers, right to send a letter of grievance to London and another, more in sorrow than in anger, to his former boss: "You are one of those unfortunate men who will have many an acquaintance, but never a real friend."

In this way the Company trained up one of the rival Syndicate's most brilliant explorers, the world's greatest land geographer of British race.

The mountain country was filling up with a terrible array of Scotchmen, all lordly Nor'Westers.

McGillises, McKays, McLellans, McDougalls, McMillans – at Hogmanay Indian braves fled in panic from their fierce and bestial potations. The region was known as New Caledonia – but here was no sabbath, no dominie, no God or devil.

Syndicate capos did not come tougher than Simon Fraser. Blooded in strong-arm clashes with rival traders, he was an illiterate, ill-bred, fault-finding jock.

Now, in 1808, he was charged with exploring the Columbia to the ocean. His canoes were efficient but far from happy ships, wrenched by the eddies and whirlpools of the worst river Fraser had ever travelled, a roystering torrent that roared and boiled in deep sunless canyons. He drove his paddlers and Indians over portages so rocky a pair of good shoes did not last out a day. And like Wee Sandy, Fraser knew nothing of Wordsworth.

Romantic scenery? He had never clapped eyes on anything so dreary and dangerous. Every way he looked, mountains upon mountains, their summits covered with eternal snow, closed the gloomy scene.

Not till he reached tidewater did he realize his mistake.

This was not the Columbia.

All unaware, he had descended the Fraser.

The Beaver Club, Montreal, 1808.

This was where they came to celebrate, the Syndicate's fur barons and Hyperborean nabobs. They liked to show off their money. In Scotch hands, the French policy of premiums and home delivery had paid off.

The Marquis was dead. But Jimmy McGill was here tonight and Alexander Henry as vice-president. Wullie McKay was cork.

Among the guests was John Jacob Astor, one of the sharpest Yanks that ever came out of Germany. He watched, calculating. Four years from now, his boys would be trading on the Pacific.

The Yanks had been slow to match Mackenzie's transcontinental march. Lewis and Clark had returned from the Coast only two years ago, claiming everything in sight.

The Syndicate drank like thirsty bears.

For dinner there was roast beaver, pemmican, sturgeon, and wild rice, followed by cheese.

Yorkshire Joe Frobisher proposed the toasts: The Mother of All the Saints, the King, the fur trade in all its branches, *voyageurs*, wives, children, and absent members.

Then they got down to serious drinking.

The night, with its drunken vistas, yawned before them.

Soon they were in full cry. The walls, the city itself with its snow-covered roofs and steeples, dissolved in clouds of alcoholic vapour and they were out in the vast night of the Northwest boozing themselves witless in silent forests. Presently their ears were amazed at the wild, lost music of the Hebrides, the skirl of warpipes in sprightly strathspey.

Nimble feet were flying among glasses and silver on the polished ma-hogany table, the dancer's eyes glazed in frenzy. Flushed nabobs banged the table and whooped their applause. Then, thinking about those who had paddled them and their fortunes over many a swift river and shining lake, they grew sentimental and filled their lungs to sing:

> 'Y a longtemps que je t'aime,
> Jamais je ne t'oublierai!

Och, aye, the *voyageurs*! Where would they be without those wee coolies, sae strong, sae cheerful, sae underpaid!

All over the old town the clocks were chiming four.

And they were doing the *grand voyage*, the whole savage brotherhood hunkered in two rows on the carpet, paddling their ghostly canoe with swords, pokers, fire-tongs, walking-sticks, singing to keep time, singing to blow away the fogs of Bacchus, the mists of creeping old age. No weather, no water – not Acheron itself – would ever stop the paddles or the song.

9.

In which the
Earl of Selkirk
founds a settlement by
the Red River.....
&
the Nor'Westers fight back

Thomas Douglas, fifth Earl of Selkirk, Baron Daer and Shortcleugh, knew Byron and was a close friend of Sir Walter Scott. Romantic was his urge to relieve the wretched clansmen his own class had dispossessed. Like Moses in a kilt, he would lead them to the Promised Land.

While he was at it, he would lead the wretched Irish too.

Arthur Dobbs's quaint notion that the prairies were fit for white settlement seemed to make sense now. And Selkirk, fresh from his triumph in peopling Prince Edward Island with Scotch ancestors, was just the lord to organise it.

The site that interested him – in the region of the Red and Assiniboine Rivers – was in Company territory. He and his brother-in-law bought enough shares to earn them influence in its policy.

They picked a good year to do it. In 1808 the Company was drifting rudderless. Competition from the Syndicate had stunned it. That arch-fiend Bonaparte had closed the continental fur markets. Though Their Honours had resisted Syndicate moves to buy them out, the value of their shares was falling. In 1809 they declared no dividend.

That year Selkirk's brother-in-law Andrew Colvile joined the Committee. He and Selkirk took hold with a firm grip – himself with his balance sheets, the earl with his Gothic schemes.

The Company ceded a hundred and sixteen thousand square miles of prairie for a token payment of ten shillings. In return for this realm of Assiniboia, Selkirk would supply settlers, food, land for retired servants, and a steady supply of vassals for the Company.

The Nor'Westers were alarmed. Settlers and trade could not mix. Farmers would drive out hunters. Worse, this settlement would be smack across their canoe routes, straddling the main river arteries and the buffalo country yielding pemmican for their Athabasca brigades.

The Syndicate now controlled the Canadas. Their boys were everywhere. Wullie McGillivray, their sweet-talking czar, was in the Executive Council – honoured as the Honourable. Friends and partners packed juries, sat on the bench, wined and dined the Governor-General. In the Upper Country, squads of their bullyboys enforced their slightest caprice. Far off in London, they had the fix in at the Colonial Office, where Lord Secretary Bathurst's chief underthing was their eager toady.

They had conquered a wilderness empire and they meant to keep it. No Saxon Charter would stand in their way, no trading lord or bible peer.

They bought out the *Inverness Journal* to run poison-pen articles slandering the projected colony and its noble patriarch. They bought Company shares and opposed Selkirk at its General Court. They harrassed embarking emigrants. They discovered a new tenderness for the rights of their drudges the Canadians, and of the Métis, their neglected offspring of the Plains.

But Selkirk was a belted Earl, a black Douglas, his motto: *Jamais arrière*. He had put on the helmet of faith, the breastplate of hope, the whole armour of righteousness. Proof against calumny, he would not, could not unbend.

Thus it was that the sea-divided Gael came to the smiling meadows of the prairies. O heart-bitter wound! Sore oppressed as they had ever been in their native shieling, that suffering was no more than the sting of a gnat to what they would endure under the vast, glaring, hostile, cloud-laden sky of this alien land. *Ochone* and alas! Cheerless and bleak as had been their lot in the windy glens of Caledonia and the remote fastness of sorrowful Erin, more bleak and cheerless yet was the doom they would endure in this new home. My grief and my sorrow! Cruel the telling! It was more than the sea divided the Gael, more than the ocean, more than the wide, gray, restless, widow-making Atlantic that empties the mind of reason – as learned Brenan said of Spanish Galicia – and fills it with bad poetry. Not the seas, not the skies divided the Gaels, but their own proud, stiff-necked hearts!

Two Scots for a drinking-bout; three for a controversy; four or more for a blood feud.

And that this pleasant, fertile, flower-painted place, well watered and cheery with voices of little feathered warbling songsters, might seem the true Eden, the very Paradise they had dreamed of in dreams and heard of in sermons, they had brought hither the Serpent – the ever-smiling, subtle, ever-watchful Campbell who would betray them!

Ah, Douglas! Och, Macdonell! What madness winkered you, what darkness of the mind and memory, that in the testing hour of danger you disremembered the Massacre of Glencoe?

Soon, too soon – evil to relate! – the valiant hand of Gael would be raised against valiant Gael, Scot against Scot, Macdonell against Macdonell, cousin against cousin. For as in far distant moors and rocky defiles clansmen did not scruple to send cruel Saxons against clansmen, so here on the boundless plains would the petty lairds and lickspittles of the Syndicate, veiling their treachery with sighs and lawsuits, set bloodthirsty half breeds upon their innocent brothers!

Little did the stout crofters of Selkirk's advance party know of all this that crystal day in Autumn, 1812. Their grief and their trouble seemed all behind them.

On the fourth day of September, Governor Miles Macdonell took formal seizin of Lord Selkirk's lands at the forks of the Red and Assiniboine rivers.

The sun shone, the flag fluttered up the mast, the escort presented arms. Macdonell read a proclamation in English and French.

Crofters fired the two brass cannon they had boated and man-hauled all the cruel way from Hudson Bay.

The natives were friendly – a handful of Indian and Métis onlookers. Even the Nor'Westers from nearby Fort Gibraltar were friendly. The gentleman in charge was Alexander Macdonell, their own Governor's cousin.

Aye – these Nor'Westers seemed a sight more friendly than the Company men up on the Bay, whose grudging hospitality the settlers had endured through a terrible winter.

A comforting illusion! The Syndicate, did they but know it, was merely biding its time, waiting for an excuse to strike and destroy them.

And Macdonell was the laddie to give it to them.

He had a passion for pemmican. For breakfast, pemmican; a smear of pemmican on the bread for elevenses; pemmican *à la King* for luncheon; hot buttered pemmican-scones with his tea; and for dinner, roast ribs of pemmican with all the trimmings. A wee supper of pemmican giblets was his bedward thought, and beside his rude four-poster, for midnight snacks, what did he keep but a dish of pemmican cold cuts?

Soon Miles Macdonell had bought up all the pemmican in Assiniboia.

The Nor'Westers liked pemmican too – but this was disgusting. Even cousin Sandy turned against Miles.

And when Miles posted a proclamation solemnly prohibiting the export of pemmican from the settlement, the Honourable Wullie McGillivray sent word from Fort William headquarters: the colony must be destroyed.

Miles had given a Disgust.

The Pemmican War was on.

"So here is at them," wrote cousin Sandy to his chieftain, "with all my heart & energy!"

His sidekick Duncan Cameron put on the scarlet of a captain in the disbanded Voyageur Corps and strutted sweatily among the Indians and Métis, inciting them to violence. The Indians, disliking treachery, would have nothing to do with it. But the Métis, troubled with an obscure sense of grievance, listened.

To the settlers Cameron offered a Gaelic mix of bribe and threats. Direct assault was too risky while they had howitzers and field-pieces in their newly built Fort Douglas. The phony captain would have to find a fifth columnist to help disarm them.

Governor Miles had gone south to Pembina to sample pemmican. In his absence, Cameron managed to find and subvert his Judas – a Campbell.

George Campbell later accepted one hundred pounds from the Syndicate for his help in stealing the guns.

A Syndicate magistrate meanwhile issued a warrant for Miles Macdonell's arrest on charges of pemmican-theft. On the understanding that the colony would not be molested, Macdonell gave himself up.

Disarmed and leaderless, the settlement was now helpless. Crofters began to leave. All too soon, a frightened remnant was fleeing the ravaged fields and burning homesteads.

A thoughtful Syndicate had arranged transportation.

Métis rode down the crops. Whooping, they galloped from house to house, leaving all in flames.

Lord Selkirk's dream was going up in smoke.

This moving Ceremony
Sketched by mee at
Ft. Douglas on the East
Bank of the Red River.
Septr. 4th 1812.
R. Searle
– in Homage to my Lord Selkirk)

The victims could not know that help was on the way.

White spray was flying from vermilion paddles, one hundred strong, of the Company's first canoe brigade racing up river from Montreal under former Nor'Wester Colin Robertson.

From the Bay, reinforcements of Highland crofters sweated their heavy York boats inland under command of no less a dignitary than the Company's new Governor-in-Chief, Robert Semple.

Vengeance is mine, saith the Lord. What was good for one lord was good enough for another. Selkirk himself, embattled scion of Archibald Bell-the-Cat, had girded himself for rescue and begun the long voyage from Britain.

By Spring 1816 – the following year – a gallant new settlement had sprung, a tender Phoenix, from the charred ruins of the old.

Colin Robertson had seized the Nor'Westers Fort Gibraltar – surprising Duncan Cameron in the act of penning his appeal for Indian attacks on the settlers: "Not that I would wish them to Butcher anyone *God forbid.*" Another jubilant letter told of the fate of Robertson's own brigade which had gone on to the Athabasca country. Thanks to the Nor'Westers, sixteen of his men had starved to death.

Taking Cameron with him under arrest, Robertson set out for York Factory and the courts of England. He was sick of quarreling crofters.

At his masthead, he flew a pemmican-sack.

Robert Semple took over.

New to the fur trade, he was a Loyalist refugee from the neighbour Republic who had seen many lands.

For all his travels, he could not get it through his head that there were places where British fair play was unheard of – and that this was one of them.

On June 19, 1816, Métis horsemen were reported gathering a little up river. Semple called for volunteers to go out with him and see what those fellows wanted.

They could talk the whole thing over.

Accompanied by a party of twenty-six or twenty-seven, he found the horsemen at a place called Seven Oaks – just off Main Street, Winnipeg, if only he had known.

The proud Ishmaels of the plains were armed, stripped for war, hideously painted like Indians.

Menacing, they fanned out in crescent as for a buffalo hunt. Backing toward the river, Semple's men straggled into line.

They had lived with fear for months. Now the crisis was on them they wished they were back with good old fear.

Here and there a war whoop went up as the crescent closed in.

Seven Oaks

Suddenly one of the horsemen broke ranks, waving his arm as he advanced on the Governor.

"What do you want?" he called.

"What do you want?" Semple shouted back.

Neither knew what he wanted.

Tension grew as the horseman came close to Semple.

No one would remember exactly what happened next. Something – some word or gesture of the Governor's – alarmed the Métis.

There was a storm of shots as they gunned the settlers down. Maddened with bloodlust, they leaped from their mounts to finish off the wounded.

When word of the massacre reached cousin Sandy Macdonell at Portage La Prairie, he was overjoyed.

"Holy Name of God!" he shouted in French. "Good news – twenty-two English killed!"

Wolves and coyotes devoured the remains.

The news reached Selkirk at Sault Sainte Marie.

He had come out of the East; he rode fully armed, nor did he ride all alone. Romantic he might be, but he was also Scotch.

The Governor-General had refused him troops. So he had raised and equipped his own regiment of Swiss gnomes – the famous Demurring Regiment.

Borrowing a trick from the competition, he had also had himself sworn in as a magistrate.

The Swiss gnomes captured Fort William without a shot fired. They sealed up offices and files.

His Lordship arrested the Honourable Wullie and his partners on charges of treason, conspiracy, and murder. He granted bail when they promised, on their word of honour as gentlemen, not to tamper with evidence.

That was only one of his many mistakes. The Syndicate were not gentlemen.

They spent a gleeful night breaking seals and burning papers.

But Selkirk had already secured clear evidence of their complicity in the Massacre of Seven Oaks and numerous other crimes.

He sent them back to the Canadas for trial. Then he went on to Red River to restore peace and order to the colony.

Selkirk knew by now that he was dealing with a Syndicate of lawless and ruthless racketeers. The fur trade was Their Thing. They ran it with a unique blend of suavity and violence. What the noble Earl did not realize was the extent to which they had involved the whole Establishment of the Canadas in Their Thing.

Selkirk

Fighting like wolves at bay, the Nor'Westers showed that they still had teeth. They had already flung a future bishop into the battle. The Right Reverend-to-be, John Strachan, a former Aberdeen Calvinist, was living high on the Anglican hog he hoped to see established in Upper Canada. He had been roused to write a scurrilous pamphlet against Selkirk.

Now the Syndicate called in other mouthpieces, their lawyers and judges.

Writs, warrants, summonses, pleadings issued in devil's plenty from their normally lethargic offices. Obstruction met Selkirk's every move to bring offenders to justice. Witnesses disappeared. Venues were shifted from province to province.

Not one of the Seven Oaks murderers – or of the Nor'Westers who had set them on and rewarded them – was ever brought to trial.

Though Selkirk had struck the Syndicate a blow from which it would never recover, its lawyers managed to drag him through the courts till his health and fortune were in ruins.

The Countess of Selkirk was bitter. "Who would have believed," she wrote, "that the mere scum of Scotland could have attained to this!"

The antagonists fought to the death. Selkirk died, in 1820, appropriately of tuberculosis. The North West Company died in 1821 of a merger with the Hudson's Bay Company.

Once more the Bay route to the fur country had proved cheaper and more efficient than the river route.

And now the Syndicate men were going straight. Overnight, the former crooks and assassins had become pillars of virtue – sober, honest, industrious. Henceforth all fur traders would be Company men as well as Scots.

The game of Monopoly was on again.

But Selkirk had planted at Red River the seeds of its ruin. With settlement would come free enterprise.

10.

In which Governor George Simpson rules over an Empire from Labrador to the Pacific

In her way Margaret Taylor was a superior female, her father a Company sea captain. That kept it in the family. *Oor ain fishguts to oor ain sea-maws*, as the factors liked to say. And she was the mother of some of his children. Which, of course, did not mean he had to marry her. Not that he had anything against wedlock – he had often wished his own parents had tried it. It was just that he was too busy.

He watched her pour tea for his breakfast. Travel kept him too busy even for her. No doubt she would get into mischief in his absence. He had no illusions about that – or about anything else for that matter. But it irked him.

He jumped up from the table, pulling on his boots, a whirlwind of energy. Next moment he was gone, heading for his cold dip. The private side-door – specially made for his Indian girls – slammed behind him.

For the present there was nothing more to do in York Factory, now the main depot supplying scores of inland posts. One of these days he would go to London to find a wife suitable to his station. But first he must inspect the Oregon country.

He gasped, splashing in icy water.

"Where the devil's my piper?"

"Play!" George Simpson said.

There was not a breath left in the boy's lungs. Where was he? In the splendid cariole with its matched team and liveried coachmen? The hot plain, choking on the dust of wild cavalry? Or running behind the glamorous sled with its pedigree Huskies? It seemed he was in full Highland costume. He had come so far and so fast he had lost all sense of place.

He concentrated on the nape of the Governor's short, thick neck just in front of him. They were in the express canoe. The York boats now replacing canoes all over the vast territory were too slow for the Governor. This gaudy, graceful craft was his favourite.

"Ah'm just a piper!" the boy croaked.

"Then pipe!"

He piped. No one argued with the Little Emperor.

As an enemy put it: "In no colony subject to the British Crown is there to be found an authority so despotic as is at this day exercised in the mercantile Colony of Rupert's Land; an authority combining the despotism of military rule with the strict surveillance and mean parsimony of the avaricious trader. From Labrador to Nootka Sound the unchecked, uncontrolled will of a single individual gives law to the land."

Simpson had earned his power. Not by military force, though. Apart from his own quick fists, dazzle and daring were his weapons. And ruthless efficiency.

Nepotism had given him his chance. His uncle a partner in one of Andrew Colvile's enterprises, Simpson began his career in the London counting-house. There he had learned to share Colvile's faith in the balance sheet.

His chance came against ferocious competition in the Athabasca country. He came out with resounding profits, his Nor'Wester opponent terrorized.

Colvile had reorganized the Company to give men on the spot a stake in its success. Chief Traders and chief factors now shared in profits and had a voice in council. They were the most formidable group of men the fur trade had ever seen.

From the start, the Little Emperor dominated them.

They were fascinated by the man, the toughest traveller of them all, breaking record after record for speed and endurance. This 1828 trip was his second to the Pacific coast. He would cover seven thousand miles in a single season.

With amazing tact and cunning he had reconciled former enemies. Cuthbert Grant, a leader of the Seven Oaks murderers, he had tamed with the flattering sinecure of Warden of the Plains. More sophisticated hoodlums were cut down to size.

The Governor kept on the move. The "most triffling information" was useful. It could be acquired only by a personal survey of the country.

Piping away like a madman, Colin Fraser watched him.

He was writing in his red leather notebook again, oblivious of the brown torrent racing between high wet cliffs, hurling them down river. The gay skirling of the pipes contended with the roar of approaching white water.

In the midst of this tumult, the Governor was keeping tabs on his men. One by one they came under sardonic scrutiny. A Chief Trader had been praised for sobriety, a great tea drinker in a country plagued with drunks. Simpson was unimpressed. "Were he to drink a pint of Wine with his Friends on extraordinary occasions, get up earlier in the morning, eat a hearty breakfast and drink less Tea I should have a much better opinion of him." A Chief Factor had shown himself a friend to generous causes. Simpson noted: "Would be a Radical in any Country under any Government."

The Indian canoe men were pale. Only their greater dread of Simpson overcame their terror of this river.

The Governor foresaw that the Yanks would get the Oregon country south of the forty-ninth parallel. He wanted to find a river route to the coast this side of the probable border. He had been told this river was too savage for trade, but had insisted on a personal inspection.

Once he reached the ocean he would admit he had been lucky to make it.

The Fraser was just as bad as he had been led to expect.

Vancouver Island and the Pacific coast were supplied by sea *via* Cape Horn. Ships of various nations had nosed in to explore its fjords and sounds and trade with its highly civilized Indians for sea-otter. Courtly British and Spanish, lantern-jawed Yanks, hairy beasts of Russian capitalist-monopolists. In the resulting free-for-all the otter were all but exterminated.

The Nor'Westers outstayed all comers.

The Indians had acquired certain novelties. Chinook love fever, as it was called, was one. And because their languages were so many and various, a new trading jargon had sprung up – a linguistic stew of Scotch, French, Indian, and other words. They spoke it with a *hee-hee tumtum* (a merry heart).

The Honourable Company fell heir to all this – especially to one Indian institution which was to prove useful in its department stores.

The coastal Indians lived in fine cedar houses and advertised their ancestry with elegant heraldic poles. They threw lavish parties at which they proved their hospitality by giving away everything they owned. In their eagerness to impress guests, they ruined themselves.

The custom was known as the potlatch. In time it caught on with the white settlers. Every Christmas they stormed the Company's department stores for goods to give away in the potlatch, to the merry ringing of cash registers.

All this was still in the future when George Simpson breathed the damp green airs of the Pacific coast.

He was appalled at the indolence and luxury of his commissioned gentlemen. They were sailing boats for pleasure! They were stuffing themselves with imported delicacies, spoiling their women with expensive perfume, gloves, ostrich feathers. They might as well be eating gold.

Everything here was on the grand scale – the mountains, the rivers, the drinking. Everything except the trade.

Nabobs trembled as their Little Emperor hammered home his policy: "Strict economy, great regularity, the comfort and convenience of the natives, the improvement of the Country, and the most minute attention to every branch of the business."

And then, as suddenly and splendidly as he had arrived, he was gone, to the thunder of saluting cannon, the sneer and snarl of lamenting pipes. Gone to inspect the posts in Alaska and to begin, from Vladivostok, his four-thousand-mile trek across Siberia to Moscow.

Long after he had left their shores, the factors in their lonely outposts were troubled with twinges of guilt. And like the mists that strayed down from the headlong tumble of mountains, an insidious sense of persecution clung about their thoughts.

Easterners did not understand.

The men on the coast were left to their own devices. In a region of temperate rain forest, characters luxuriated like fantastic vegetation.

One of them, James Douglas – a former Nor'Wester – became the Father of British Columbia. He achieved it in the same casual way as fur-traders did other kinds of paternity.

Deciding in 1849 to found a colony on Vancouver Island, the British Colonial Office sent out Richard Blanshard as Governor.

Afflicted with a grievous tic, the young man found himself representing Queen Victoria without salary, police, law officers, army, or jail. And apart from a single crazy settler there was no one to govern. Company men took their orders from James Douglas, their dour Chief Factor. Blanshard found himself very much an outsider. After less than two years he quit.

Though still Chief Factor, Douglas was appointed his successor.

He complained of the conflict of interest.

But seeing he was stuck with the job, he decided to make the best of it.

He appointed a council to advise him. All were Company or ex-Company men. He made his brother-in-law Chief Justice and settled back to enjoy himself.

When disaffected settlers complained of his Company Family Compact, he set up an elected assembly. Every member elected was a Company man.

Racked with recurring gold fever and fears of Yankee annexation, the infant colony led an uneasy existence. As always, fur interests clashed with those of settlers. Yet by the late 1850's Victoria, the colonial capital, was a bustling seaport and the Company store had to face competition from Lester and Gibbs – rivals who were not only American but black.

Following a gold rush to Fraser river, Douglas took over on the mainland, protecting British – and Company – sovereignty.

In 1858, Douglas was appointed first Governor of the new crown colony of British Columbia. He resigned from the fur trade.

But the future Sir James kept his flair for judicial appointments.

Matthew Baillie Begbie, his most striking choice, was a judge who thought he had a way with juries. At least one jury disappointed him. Ignoring his charge, they acquitted a man accused of murder, finding him guilty of manslaughter only.

Begbie, enraged, told the prisoner he deserved to be hanged. Then, turning on the twelve good men and true, he roasted them.

"And you, gentlemen of the jury, you are a pack of Dalles horse thieves, and permit me to say it would give me great pleasure to see you hanged, each and every one of you!"

England was reforming. The right little, tight little island, with its rotten boroughs, its hanging judges, and gin-shops was becoming the earnest metropolis of empire. A new seriousness was in the air as Methodists weaned the savage population from rotgut spirits to wholesome beer and tea.

The slave trade which had fattened generations of Liverpool merchants would not be outlawed till 1843. But liberty was the coming thing, a new, heady ideal to brighten the sabbath glooms of Victoria's long reign.

Monopoly was growing unpopular. Adam Smith's dismal science taught that commercial health could be won only in a free market. Belief in free trade was becoming a dogma. In the 1840's millions of famished Irish would be sacrificed to it.

With grave misgivings Parliament had extended the trading monopoly after the Company had swallowed its great rival, renewing it with fresh doubts in 1839.

But fur trade experience did seem to show that free competition was destructive of the Indians. It had led to violence, lavish abuse of liquor, and over-trapping. Only a monopoly could keep the peace, enforce conservation, and cut down on liquor.

More than anything, it was fear of the demon alcohol that inspired Parliament to renew the monopoly. The spectre of lives wrecked by cheap spirits was very real in Britain, and reformers all hated liquor. Not till the 1890's would a serious-minded intellectual defend the use of spirits as trade goods. In West Africa, Mary Kingsley was to argue that contempt for natives underlay prohibitionism.

The Indians, at all events, bitterly resented having their booze cut off. When Beaver Indians were refused a drink at a Company post in the Peace River country, they killed the offending white men. The Little Emperor responded by closing the shop. The Beaver moved on to harrass other posts.

The Canadas, too, were reforming. Radical Jack Durham had come and gone and let off his famous Report. And the Family Compact, bloated heirs to the Syndicate, found themselves confronted by tight-lipped, chapel-going democrats – "damned cold water drinking Methodists," as Colonel Talbot called them.

Upper Canadians coveted the Red River colony. They wanted to be populous enough to dominate Lower Canada, whose exploding population frightened them.

Montrealers resented the loss of the fur trade. Worse, Simpson was replacing their paddlers with Iroquois.

At Red River and on the coast, settlers were becoming impatient with Company rule. The Company seemed to care more about Indians and beavers than they did about farmers and Swiss watch-makers.

Parliament ends trading monopoly

All these misgivings and resentments culminated in the Parliamentary Inquiry of 1857.

Once again the secretive functionaries of the Honourable Company found themselves naked to the world.

The Little Emperor was summoned to the bar of Parliament and subjected to cross-examination by known radicals. He did not like it one bit.

In his seventies now, he was a rich old satrap who had never in his long reign lost sight of the first principle of empire – profit. Year after year he had kept the dividends rolling in for the British proprietors. Long since he had pensioned off his old concerns to marry a pretty young cousin. In 1841, Queen Victoria had knighted him for his services to Arctic exploration.

Compared to Sir George Simpson, other empire builders are mere pussy-cats. Beside him, Rhodes is a reed, Lugard a laggard, Wellington a wornout boot. Yet he had never become a hero of the middle class. There were no Simpson anecdotes in the children's story books, no hysterical crowds to greet his arrival in the capital. And now he was on the mat, his whole life's work called in question.

The fur trade was dying. The silk hats on his inquisitors were proof of it. He himself was a relic of a tougher, more cynical age.

In reply to Lord Stanley's question about the Columbia district, he said shortly, "I think there is no portion of that country north of forty-nine degrees adapted for settlement."

And to Mr. Grogan: "The Country is not favourable for settlement, I think, about Red River."

He meant it. Floods, locusts, and other disasters had made the place intolerable.

But these gentlemen were quoting his own travel-book to him, a lot of lyrical stuff about alluvial soil and so forth. He should never have hired that ghost-writer.

It was Edward Ellice, M.P., an old Nor'Wester, who best put the Company's position. The Company did not profit from its efforts at government in the new settlements. Its administrative work was much more important to Canada and England than to itself.

The Parliamentary report cleared the way for the next stride towards a chain of department stores.

Parliament had begun to dismantle the great trading monopoly.

London, late in 1862. A single ray of sunlight, pale and sickly after its struggle through December fog and the grimy windows of Hudson's Bay House on Fenchurch Street, fell on Prince Rupert's clean cut cheek in the fine Lely portrait.

The visitors noticed it at once – the one hint of youth in this dark, dirty, cavernous room. All else whispered of decrepit old age and neglect: the faded green cloth, blackened rheumaticky chairs, floor-boards that wheezed underfoot, the very air that seemed to have been shut in for centuries with its memories.

Most elderly of all, older than he or anyone else cared to remember, Governor Henry Hulse Berens, supported by two hardly less ancient Committeemen – like a dying pope flanked by senile chamberlains – glowered at the intruders with undisguised suspicion.

The Duke of Newcastle (he was Colonial Secretary) had introduced them, a group of British bankers and financiers chattering about roads, telegraphs, and whatnot. Like the Duke himself, they seemed to have dangerously extended ideas.

The visitors moved cautiously, awkwardly conscious of their own energy. These men were the future, pulsing with the heartless optimism of machines. Steam, gentlemen! they seemed to be saying as they consulted their gold watches, steam! – as they worked their elbows like pistons – steam will blow you, puff! into oblivion.

The railway-promoter fellow, Edward Watkin, looked Berens in the eye. The old gentleman felt a fleeting chill. He could have sworn he saw steam coming out of the fellow's ears.

He rallied.

"It is a question, my dear sir, of a million and a half of money." Berens' tone was just short of insulting. "Cash."

The visitors smiled. There would be no difficulty, then.

Watkin would inspect the accounts. The finance company would put up the money.

When the deal went through in 1863, the Company's old men felt they had sold out at a capital price. And the new men had acquired all the land they needed for railways, telegraph, roads.

For the gentlemen in London it was a splendid bargain.

News of the takeover reached far-off posts and forts by sea, by express canoe, by crack dog team.

The factors struck their brows.

"We have been sold out like cattle," they said.

The new men had bigger things to think about. To save the Grand Trunk Railway from bankruptcy, it must be extended from the Canadas coast to coast. Two-way traffic would reduce ruinous overheads. The line would run through Company territory close to the United States – leaving the Shield to the fur trade. The prairies and the Pacific coast would fill up with settlers loyal to the Queen and Empire.

Financiers and politicians went impatiently to work, planning the long string of railway stations known as Confederation.

In 1867 the British North America Act established the Dominion of Canada.

The rest was for phrase-makers, *a mari usque ad mare*.

The new men had a nightmare. They had created a monster. The newborn nation was brusquely demanding that the Company surrender its remaining rights under the Charter.

It was 1869.

D'Arcy McGee materialized, all Irish smiles – but swinging a shilelagh.

"Arrah, be aisy, boys," this Father of Confederation was saying. "Lie down and let me knock your brains out."

They lay down and let him knock their brains out.

This was known as the Deed of Surrender. And a fearsome deed it was.

For three hundred thousand pounds the Company ceded the whole of Rupert's Land, nearly a million and a half square miles of territory which it had owned and governed for two hundred years.

The Company retained forty-five thousand acres around its hundred and twenty forts and posts. In time it received an additional seven million acres of settlement land.

The neighbour Republic kicked through with four hundred and fifty thousand dollars in payment for the Oregon country.

Smith. What could one do with a name like Smith?

Year after year Donald Smith brooded on this problem in the wilderness of Labrador. He was Scotch, he was a Company man, compulsive thrift was in his bones. He saved what he might have spent on razors by letting his beard grow long and white and venerable. He saved nails as they came out of Company crates and sorted them in his spare time. He saved his share of fur profits till the new finance-company men put an end to profit-sharing.

In Montreal, a tiger among bulls and bears, he played the market with his savings. By his forties he was rich.

And still he was stuck with this name.

"Don't brood," Mrs. Smith said. "You'll get a coronary."

It came to him then. Not coronary but coronet! A title! In London you could get knighted, barted, ennobled. With this beard, that bank balance, those mink-lined connections, he was halfway to duke already.

Thus by saving and sorting nails the good man succeeded in changing his name to Strathcona. He became Governor of the Company, so deeply revered that when the empire went to war in South Africa, he was allowed to send out his favourite horse at his own expense. For years grateful South Africans would remember Lord Strathcona's horse.

But first he served Canada and the Company.

It was not just Company men who were shocked by the Deed of Surrender. The Métis were disgusted too. No one had thought to ask them if they wanted to be handed over to Canada. Since they had always hated change, they opted for revolution.

Smith, as Canada's commissioner, went to Red River in 1869 and persuaded them to keep the peace. It was not his fault that Riel, the Métis leader, later changed his mind and launched an insurrection.

When the Canadian Pacific Railway ran out of money before it had run out of country, Strathcona put his hand in his own pocket for the difference. He drove the last spike himself.

Under Strathcona's guidance the Company made huge profits from land deals, earning money but losing friends, while the fur trade dwindled.

The Company had founded the cities of Winnipeg, Edmonton, Victoria, and others in the West. New towns were springing up along the railway. Strathcona failed to notice that swarms of a new breed of customer were clamouring to be served. They wore white stetsons, chewed tobacco, and kept brass spittoons in the front room. But they also kept a whole army of energetic retailers in business.

Where were the long-awaited department stores of the Bay?

11.

In which Their Honours at last succeed in establishing a chain of department stores.

They did not begin to appear till the second decade of the twentieth century. They were splendid when they came, in the heroic style demanded by the well-heeled citizenry of what Sir Wilfrid Laurier had promised would be Canada's century.

In the downtown centres of western cities still scaled to the leisurely clop-clop of surrey and victoria, Bay stores sprang up to challenge the now formidable competitors.

Here at last was the late-blooming flower of the Honourable Company, a chain of emporiums selling goods of a luxury to scandalize Governor Bayly's Quaker heart: hardware and textiles, furniture and drugs, bibles and band instruments and boots, candies and carpets and jewels and toys – the whole prodigal potlatch of an endlessly inventive industrial revolution. And along with the goods came no less inventive services: credit branching into ingenuities no Orkneyman ever dreamed of, counselling, warranties, home delivery, repairs, parking – and above all, considering the Methodist competition, probity.

Merchandizing became show business, the department store a glamorous midway of conspicuous consumption, a dazzling circus of display and opulence. The ferris wheel of fashion turned, glittering. Here the affluent society crowded daily to view itself in a thousand mirrors, honouring itself in an ever-renewed fiesta of buying and spending, ringing up the sales, bringing in the sheaves, wearing down the shoes.

It was the age of the salesman. Smiling ribbon clerks had replaced the Scotch gunpowder shark.

In the long pause of Depression and World War the salesman wilted. Before he knew it, gorgeous sales girls were whirling him into the marketing revolution that followed the impact of television.

Bay stores pursued their automobile-borne customers to the new suburbs and shopping plazas, carrying them by escalator to unprecedented heights of ecstatic spending. By the late 1960's there were Bay stores everywhere in Canada. The circus of commerce was gayer and louder, more pop, gear, groovy, as the world's oldest merchandizing corporation learned to swing.

In more than two hundred Northern Stores the fur trade was still alive. Wild furs were still taken, but more often Eskimos came to the Bay to *buy* dressed wolfskins for parka trimmings.

A vast new industry of fur ranching was served by the Company's great auction houses in Montreal, New York, and London. In the shadow of Committeeman Wren's great monument of St. Paul's, white-coated buyers from all over the world thronged Beaver Hall. There was no candle burning now, but the smell of the raw pelts was the old familiar one. It was the same in Montreal and Manhattan – the overpowering odour of pelts, the hypnotic chant of auctioneers.

One of the Company's first clerks had written, carefully, at the head of each page of his accounts: "*Laus Deo* In London." Praise God, in London. And in the City of London, within sound of Bow Bells, the head office had remained for three centuries. In this maze of narrow streets, this huddle of counting houses, banks, pubs, Wren churches, were concentrated some of the shrewdest commercial brains in the world. This has homburg and bowler territory, rolled umbrella country: hats and noses were hard, ferrules and wits sharp. But the City had its own style and tradition; power was tempered by civility. The Hudson's Bay Company had always been part of this London, had drawn on its talent and experience for top executives.

The premises in Great Trinity Lane had an air of thrift and elegance unique to London, smelling of raw mink, floor polish, parchment. The portrait of Sir George Simpson wore a satisfied look. Scholars visiting the archives were given tea and footnotes as they hunted through three hundred years of accounts, letters and Exact Journals for the rousing story of the far distant shops.

As the Company's third centennial approached, about ninety per cent of its stock was owned by some 32,000 proprietors in Britain. The City was still vigorously present in the Committee. Yet if the proprietors were still overwhelmingly adventurers of England, the Company's operations were just as overwhelmingly Canadian. A British company functioning almost exclusively in Canada – it meant Their Honours were leading a double life. No one actually said, "We can't go on meeting like this!" But that was what it was coming to. British domicile exposed the Company to fiscal hazards not faced by its competitors.

Not that it was easy for Canadians on the Committee to think of giving up London, the place where good Canadians went in afterlife. They knew the crumpets were browning for them on the other side, but even the scholars thought London was a long way to go for tea. In the year one thousand nine hundred and seventy, it was time to think of bringing the Company to the New World.